Learning the Ropes

Achieving Sustainable Sales Performance Regardless of Changes in Personnel

Matt Garman

Learning the Ropes

ISBN 9781999991005

Published by Matt Garman 2018
London, England UK

Author: Matt Garman

Writer: Kerry Parkinson Day

Cover Photography: Martin Lulham

Contents   Page

Acknowledgements

Everyone I've known has contributed to this book in some way because I've learnt from every experience I've ever had, good and bad, and that has made this possible.

In particular, I'm lucky to have had the benefit of John Linney's knowledge and wisdom, especially when mapping out the early versions of the methodology. At that time, we had the good fortune to have the involvement of Colin Bradbury who made sense of the ideas we fired at him, hoping he would be able to wrestle them into a workable format and he did.

I'd like to say a special thanks to all my customers and clients, many of whom have since become great friends. They've all trusted me and provided endless challenges that have shaped my thinking and sharpened my insight. The methodology developed further as a direct result of all these interactions.

Challenging the way I think has had a huge influence on who I am today. My thanks to Magda Harbour, who has helped me open my mind, accept who I am and understand what drives and motivates me.

My deepest thanks go to my family. The love I have for them is my true north, it is my joy. My wife Sam, my son Joseph and my daughter Mollie are the reason for everything I do. They believe in me even when I doubt myself, they trust me and they challenge me every day. We are Team G.

Matt Garman, Seaford, 2018

Preface

Who is this book for?

I wrote this book for MDs and CEOs, simply because they have the most to lose if their sales teams aren't functioning well and the most to gain when they are. But it's not limited to them, if you're a sales leader, a sales person or even someone who just fancies a career in sales, then there's a wealth of information here for you too.

I learnt by jumping in with both feet, taking risks and making mistakes. I hope this book will help you to avoid some of the mistakes I made, and give you a comprehensive overview of all aspects of the sales process.

I've spent over 25 years learning, developing and refining this methodology to the point where I'm confident that it will identify areas that need your attention, and show you how to fix your sales problems, whatever they are.

I started out with the confidence of someone who didn't know what they didn't know; you will have a real advantage if you know what you need to know.

So who are you?

- Chief Executive Officer
- Managing Director
- Business Leader
- Sales Leader

- Sales Executive
- An investor

You might be facing any of these challenges:

- Your sales revenue is flat lining and you can't increase it
- Your sales team are demotivated and under performing
- You have insufficient sales structure and process
- You're too reliant on one or two main players
- You and your Board have lost confidence in your sales team
- You're spinning too many plates and starting to smash a few
- Your sales leader needs extra support
- You're looking to sell your business and want to ensure it's self-sufficient
- You're having difficulty making a decision to change how you operate
- You're tolerating mediocrity at best and sub-standard at worst because you don't know what changes to make
- You worry that you don't know if you can cope with changes you need to make
- You're hesitating because fear of failure is greater than the lure of success
- A PE/VC invested business is simply not performing

This list touches on only a few of the varied challenges that can pop up in your business. There are up years when everything goes well, your company is thriving and your staff are happy and productive, then for no apparent reason, you can plunge into a down year where things miss the mark and suddenly there are problems everywhere.

Continuing analysis of your operation and consistency in your sales process will help to level out these highs and lows and set your company on a smooth incline of steady, sustainable growth and profit.

Is it magic? It may look like it, but it's actually just plain common sense.

And one more, you might've picked this up because you're a smart, young sales person in your first job, with a keen eye on your career and future promotion.

Whoever you are, this book is for you.

Enjoy!

Introduction

You'd like to think that everyone who writes a book on how to succeed in business (without really trying) has found the magic bullet and they're going to give it to you. The truth is that there isn't just one bullet there are loads. They litter the life stories of the rich and famous and the not so famous. Read any local person makes good story and you'll spot theirs. Great news, but how do you find the magic bullet that has your name on it, the one that resonates with you?

I was born with lots of gifts that I failed to recognise, because I was too busy thinking about what I didn't have and what I didn't want. I have learned that experiences make up who we are and how we think. Perspective influences what we see and never more than when we look in the mirror.

So what do I see when I look in the mirror?

Good question, honest answer is it varies. On a good day I grin, slap myself on the back and mutter to myself 'You've done well for a fisherman' and on other days I shut my eyes and can almost feel the swell of the English Channel under my feet and the stink of fish waiting to be gutted. I still struggle with imposter syndrome, but mostly I get on with it because whether I'm pretending to be brave or really am brave, what you see is the same thing. I suspect the same could be said about all of us.

The Early Years

I had a happy childhood, the middle child of three. We were all outdoorsy kids fiercely competitive, especially me, maybe because I had more to prove as the middle child.

School was not my thing, perhaps it was too hard work to 'win' or perhaps what 'winning at school' looked like wasn't clear to me. I know that if I couldn't win, I didn't want to take part and maybe I just loved rugby and fishing too much.

As my rebellious years set in, I spent a lot of time with my late uncle John who wrote and photographed for fishing and hunting magazines. I loved him and credit him with being my first real mentor, he was at the top of his game and I really looked up to him.

Much to my family's disappointment I dropped out of school at 16 and signed up to a youth training scheme to be a commercial fisherman. Even at that early stage I don't think I ever intended it to be my long-term future, but it was an adventure for a time.

I was making money and at the age of 19 with interest rates at 14.25% – I bought my first flat. That's when life got way too serious way too soon. I now needed regular money with my new responsibilities and after witnessing the burial at sea of one of the guys on another boat – I decided to quit fishing.

I needed to change some things about my life and with only a few years of life after school experience under my belt, I attended a franchise exhibition in London and got mailshotted by a life insurance business: 'run your own business without the overheads'.

I could do that! Basically it was cold calls, trying to sell life insurance – yes, I was that guy - but there was some good training so I ran with it. I can't say I liked it, but it had awoken something deep inside me, a little kernel of knowledge that I had a lot of natural selling ability that I hadn't even started to tap into.

The money was up and down and with a flat I couldn't afford I became totally skint – surviving on plain pasta with the occasional army ration pack that a pal in the army shared with me when he came to visit. I made the only decision I could – I rented out my flat to save money and moved into a room in a mate's mother's house.

It was tough swallowing my pride but it was easier than losing my flat which was my first step to the life I knew I wanted.   I realised that while I liked selling and was good at it, I hated life insurance.

My big break came with the help of a friend who recommended me to a small IT reseller who wanted a sales person – 'I'm your man' I thought, with all the arrogance of youth and the confidence of someone beginning to change their experiences, both good and bad into a valuable asset. My plan was to sell IT during the day and life insurance in the evening – this lasted two days. The new sales job hooked me and I couldn't wait to jettison the life insurance. I learned like a crazy man on a mission loving every minute – and I only worked 5 days a week now. It was commission only but guaranteed at £500 per month. I would pay the guarantee back when I sold stuff. It took me 6-9 months to build a pipeline, then I was suddenly earning more than five grand a month and didn't look back.

I was good at this, I couldn't stop selling, I had a thirst for it. For the first time in my life I wanted to learn more, I got studious about sales. I knew if I learnt more, I could earn more.

I studied, picked up experience and found new and better ways of doing things. By the time I was 30, I owned and ran the company and after increasing its sales and profits, I realised I'd reached the highest level I could with the set up at the time. The business had two divisions: software and IT, which I split into two separate entities. I sold the IT side and kept the software business, which I merged with another software company. I applied what I'd learnt and again after increasing the sales and profits, it was sold it to a company backed by private equity. I'd made it. I had money in the bank, but no purpose. I had skills and knowledge, which I was still itching to use, but suddenly, I had no direction.

Salvation came when an ex-client rang me up and asked me to 'come and beat up my sales team' – I didn't know anything about their products but he was insistent: 'No Matt, but you bloody know how to run a sales team'. And I did.

The year was 2013 and Sales Plus Profit was born.

My magic bullet was the moment I realised I could study, learn and that knowledge would set me free, not trap me like I'd felt it would at school.

When I set up Sales Plus Profit I knew I had something great to offer. I was full of experience, had all this great knowledge honed and fine-tuned over years and now I could get it out there to help businesses that were either struggling or just wanted to step up a level.

I started to put together the first pass at my sustainable sales system. It has continued to develop and has been tried and tested over many years. As with all great methodologies, while the basics will stay the same, there is plenty of room to add your own special magic to create something that works for you and complements your own style.

Whatever industry you're in, whatever you think about selling and sales, it's dead simple. Sales is mostly about systems and process.

So, here we are and without further ado. Let's begin at the very beginning.

The Four Pillars - Vision, People, Process, Management

Each of the four pillars has five steps, providing twenty possible areas that need to be examined. This will enable you to assess the potential for increasing your sales and maximising your profits. What your business needs will be identified by the information gathered when you answer the questions generated by these prompts. You should find enough information to offer solutions for any specific key issues or problems.

Vision	People	Process	Management
Alignment to Corporate Strategy	Roles and Responsibility	Sales and Marketing Alignment	Forecasting Metrics and KPIs
Value Proposition	Hiring and Onboarding	Winning New Customers	Sales Meetings and Structures
Addressable Market	Training and Development	Maximising Lifetime Value	Performance Management
Competitive Landscape	Salary Commission and Bonuses	CRM and Technology	Strategic Sales Planning
Go To Market Strategy	Culture and Knowledge Sharing	Documentation and Collateral	Integration with the Wider Business

When I worked on my own, I knew what I was doing and rarely needed to create formal documentation because it was second nature to me, born of my passion for selling and solving problems and my experience in all sorts of challenges facing different sales teams.

What I found was that although every issue is unique, it has basic elements and can be understood if the component parts are examined, much as you might take an engine apart to find which pieces are misaligned, causing it to run below its optimum performance.

Before we focus on the four pillars we need to put what we find in context. Building an executive summary – a snapshot of your company - to anchor what we find in its specific reality is the simplest way to do this.

Executive Summary:

- A high level overview of your business and its aspirations
- A comprehensive snapshot of the past/present/future of your company
- Highlights, development and growth

Topics that will help you to build the summary:

- Age/maturity of your business
- Ownership - including any changes
- Historical growth patterns
- Changes and key milestones
- Special achievements, awards and stand outs

Topics required for the summary:

- Attitude to sales within your business
- Recent performance of your sales function
- Your definition of success

Once you have your executive summary locked in, you're ready take a general look at your company's sales operation. Make it an honest appraisal – really look at it – you want to illuminate key issues that will be contributing to the company's performance both good and bad.

Your company's culture

- Is it a good place to work?
- Do your Sales Staff work as a team?
- Are they competitive/is it healthy competition?
- Is it good for the individual and good for your company?

Creativity or lack of creative thinking

- Take a look at the personalities in your company – do you have a good mix?
- What are the power shifts or struggles?
- How are internal and external advisors influencing outcomes?
- Where is your company knowledge coming from are you in control of it?
- Do you have business mentors and are they in conflict?
- Do you use 'How to' publications?
- Business Whisperers/shareholders/friends/family?

Location

- Are split locations influencing decisions?
- Are they causing disharmony due to perceived head office bias?
- Do they work against success?

Company philosophy to sales and business growth
dynamics

- Fly 'under the radar' observe your staff and inter
  company relationships
- Don't rely on what staff tell you, read the tea
  leaves
- Use your intuition to find out what the situation
  really is

When it's your own company and you're invested both
emotionally and financially, it's easy not to see what's
really there, but don't be frightened by what you learn.
This is the knowledge you need to examine properly how
and why your company is performing the way it is. This
is true whether the news is good or bad. Good you can
build to better, bad you can fix. Knowledge is your key to
unlocking your profitable future.

Now that you've got a good general overview of how the
company's tracking – it's time to get under the bonnet
and have a closer look.

Vision

Vision	People	Process	Management
Alignment to Corporate Strategy	Roles and Responsibility	Sales and Marketing Alignment	Forecasting Metrics and KPIs
Value Proposition	Hiring and Onboarding	Methodology and Winning Customers	Sales Meetings and Structures
Addressable Market	Training and Development	Maximising Lifetime Value	Performance Management
Competitive Landscape	Salary Commission and Bonuses	CRM and Technology	Strategic Sales Planning
Go To Market Strategy	Culture and Knowledge Sharing	Documentation and Collateral	Integration with the Wider Business

A clearly defined and well-articulated vision is the lifeblood of any well performing company. It outlines your targets, provides you with a sense of direction, sketches out the steps you need to take and the criteria to be met for you to reach your goals.

This is probably not new to you, but while most companies understand the importance of an overarching business vision, few take the time to provide the same organisational framework specifically for their sales processes. The disadvantage of not doing this, is the potential loss of dynamic sales and staff who are more likely to underperform and under-deliver.

It doesn't have to be that way.

A sales vision provides the same structure and inspiration to your sales team, as a company vision outlines for your entire business – but it also goes one step further. Your sales vision links your overarching goals and your sales-specific targets. It works as a GPS showing how your whole team is involved in getting you from where you are, to where you want to be.

The five key elements are:

Alignment to Corporate Strategy
- How does your Sales team operate in alignment to the wider Corporate Vision?

Value Proposition
- What is your Value Proposition and how is it presented both internally and externally?

Addressable Market
- What is the scope and size of the market in which your company, products and services operate?

Competitive Landscape
- Who are your key competitors and what are your strategies for selling against the competition?

Go to Market Strategy
- How does your Sales plan steer the Sales and Marketing efforts towards success?

Titles look good and snappy phrases sound clever and informed, but it's important to understand what they really mean and how they relate to your business. So let's take a deep dive into each of these.

Alignment to Corporate Strategy

I remember sitting in a meeting with a client and three director shareholders. They had asked for help to address a problem with their revenue that had been static for three years. After a few minutes discussing it I was confused - I couldn't work out what the issue really was, then it dawned on me that they were talking about different things. I decided to be bold and asked if I could have a chat with each of them on their own. They all looked at me a bit strangely but cautiously agreed. I asked each of them a really simple question: 'What does your company do?'
My instinct was correct – they all gave me an entirely different view:
'We're a consulting company doing...'
'We're a technology company doing...'
'We're a software company doing...'

Bottom line? They hadn't actually agreed on what their company did. Not that unusual when a group of friends or ex-colleagues get together to 'just do some stuff'. They knew there must be a better way but didn't know what it was. More importantly, there was no chance of fixing their revenue problem until they agreed what they were and where they were going. Once this was in place, we could start aligning their sales activities to their corporate objectives.

GOAL: *To investigate whether there is a clearly articulated set of corporate objectives and the extent to which they are reflected in your sales strategy.*

DISCOVERY*: Does your company articulate what you expect Sales to deliver based on corporate priorities?*

Your Corporate Vision (the 'what') needs to align with your Sales Plan (the 'how').

Vision (What):

Growth is an almost universal corporate objective but it needs to be defined more precisely if your salespeople are to understand how they can help achieve it. You might want high sales growth, high profit growth or a combination of the two.

Routes to high sales growth:

- Ensuring sales keep pace with the growth in overall demand for the product, but only if that growth is sufficient to meet your company's goals.
- If market growth is too slow, your company will need to increase its market share. Does your company recognise how this can be achieved e.g. offering Innovative products or competing In areas such as service or price?

Routes to high profit growth:

- As well as top-line growth, higher margins can drive profit growth. This can come through premium pricing and/or cost cutting.
- If you have a premium pricing strategy are your products sufficiently differentiated to support it?
- Are your salespeople armed with the arguments to justify premium prices? Are they familiar with the offerings from key competitors?
- Using aggressive pricing strategies can also drive profit growth. This can boost your top-line but at

the price of a margin hit. Has your company identified the market share target that would trigger a switch from those aggressive tactics?

Products / Services:

- Does your company offer more than one product or service and if you do, is there a strategy for each?
- Is there is a range of offerings with different Unique Selling Points (USP) and if there is, do your salespeople understand that different approaches will be needed for each?
- Is your company prioritising one product/service or giving equal weight to pushing the entire range?
- Does your product/service lend itself to the sales/profit/margin strategy you've chosen? Salespeople will struggle if a product with no clear USP is priced at a premium rate.

Customers:

- What kind of customers do you want to attract? This will depend on the value proposition and on decisions made about priorities (sales growth, margins etc.)
- Is your business chasing any potential customer or a specific type who can deliver what the business needs?
- Have you segmented customers by business activity, size or geographic location and decided which to prioritise?
- Do your team understand this when they create their prospect list and cultivate the pipeline?

Sales Plan (How):

Your sales plan should be specific about who needs to take what actions to realise your company's vision. Without a sales plan, a business vision is just a wish list.

The right sales process:

- Do your salespeople understand the corporate strategy from the moment they join your company?
- Do you have the right sales people in the right roles with the right incentives?
- Is your sales force sufficiently educated on the key product USPs to drive high volume growth?
- Do they have access to the right sales and marketing materials?
- Do they have the right technological tools?
- Do they know how much autonomy they have on pricing and are they regularly updated on your company's strategy?
- Is all this embodied in a Strategic Sales Plan?

ACTIONS:

- You must be able to answer all these questions before you can begin to attack the detail in the People, Process and Management Pillars.

- You should also consider how you communicate your corporate objectives to your sales force and management. Your board and senior management will of course know the company's corporate objectives, but unless the objectives are also fed down systematically to sales and marketing to be translated into specific action points they will be ineffective.

- When your Vision and Sales Plan are aligned, your costs will be controlled, your waste minimised, internal conflicts avoided, your resources conserved and your customer relationships will be protected.

Value Proposition

I attended a Master class a few years ago and quite early on the speaker randomly picked members of the audience and asked them to say what their value proposition was. As he went around the audience we all started to sink lower into our chairs. It was clear that although people knew what they had to offer, no one could articulate it succinctly, everyone just waffled on. Later in our workgroups we were asked to write our value propositions down. Each of us produced long paragraphs, very wordy, careful to include all we had to offer. We were all told to cut them down by half, then half again and finally to a single sentence – and that was to be as short as possible. As I stared at mine and picked out four words, I suddenly got it. I didn't need anyone to confirm it for me; I had articulated my company's value proposition. Short, sharp, clear, defined. No argument. 'We fix sales problems.'

GOAL: *To identify a clear sales proposition for each of your products or services in relation to each target customer segment.*

DISCOVERY: *Can you articulate, internally and externally, the value proposition of your products and services?*

Company value proposition:

Think about why a customer should buy from you rather than somebody else. The answer is that it's actually about more than a USP; it's about the value that your customer derives from buying your product.

- What differentiates your company and products from your competitors?
- Is it quality, innovation, price, service – and where do they fit in the market for those products?
- What does your product do for your customer? How does it make their life, or their own customer's life, easier or better?
- What's the balance between the cost of your product and the overall benefit to your customer, in essence, what is your customer's return on investment?

How well is the value proposition understood?

- Your salespeople must be able to articulate the value proposition for both your company and your products. This starts from their first day in your business.
- If different salespeople were asked about the value proposition, would they give the same answer or would they focus on the features and benefits that they believe are the most important?
- Could your salespeople tell a prospect in one sentence why your company should be considered as the vendor of choice?
- Do you train and test your salespeople for that knowledge regularly?
- Why do your customers buy from you, do you know what your customers think differentiates your products?
- Internal communication: Does the sales force have access to a written description of the value proposition?

- Are you articulating the value proposition clearly and consistently in your marketing materials?

Measuring the truth of your value proposition:

- Does your business systematically measure whether you deliver what you think you deliver?
- Do you ask your customers to quantify the value they get from your products?
- If your value proposition rests on innovative products, do you measure whether your competitors are introducing products that eat away at that?
- If it's about service, how often do you survey your customers about service quality?
- If speed of response or delivery is part of your value proposition, do you monitor it?
- If it's price, do you check regularly on your competitors pricing to ensure you still have an advantage?
- In summary, do you actually measure your value proposition?

ACTION:

Define your Value Proposition

Complete a SWOT analysis of your own products and those of your key customers.

Strengths	Weaknesses	Opportunities	Threats
Examples:	Examples:	Examples:	Examples:
Products are superior to competitors allowing premium pricing	Products vulnerable to technical advancements	New technology could give an additional edge and create new market	Rivals adjusting their product price point
Equal quality products to competitors but lower price	Vulnerable to price war, operating at margins	Competitor losing market share	Unable to defend current strengths if competitors decide to match or better offering
Better service than competitors			New entrants could erode existing loyal market

With a clear understanding of your company's value proposition, your existing customer base can be analysed and your potential customer base for your products/services can now be identified.

Understanding and Communication:

To understand how well your value proposition is known and perceived you'll need to ask your sales staff.

- Do they know what it is and can they articulate it in an 'elevator pitch'?
- Check that everyone involved in your selling process has been trained in the value proposition
- Spot check by attending prospect meetings regularly with your sales people and see if they

are actually incorporating the value proposition as a core part of their sales pitch

- Speak to or survey your customers to find out if they understand your value proposition. Don't just presume an understanding of why they buy from you, ask them

- Analyse your marketing materials. Do they reflect your value proposition?
- Do they show it has been objectively validated or are there just vague assertions about great quality/service/pricing?

It is vital to measure the factors you claim as your value proposition, without it your sales pitch is subjective and unsupported by hard evidence.

Addressable Market

The latest version of your product is so good that the phone is going to be ringing off the hook and the queue to your door is going to be longer than at an Apple launch. It's so great that all you can think of is the phrase: 'It's the best thing since sliced bread'. I've been there, felt that and it's so exciting, this is it! Everyone you meet is going to be a prospect and buy it. The reality is that they won't, because you're not Apple, and you don't have the marketing budget to address everyone. You need to reign in your enthusiasm, understand that the prospect of too much opportunity brings distraction and get back to identifying and qualifying your customer base. There's still a place for optimism and if you really have created the best thing since sliced bread, word will spread (sorry about the pun!) but you need to take it one step at the time and be realistic about the size of your universe.

GOAL: *To identify and quantify the potential customer base for your company's products.*

DISCOVERY: *Realistically, what is the size of the universe of customers that you can reach?*

When you invest in manufacturing a product or create a service, you need to know the realistic size of your potential market. A good grasp of the market size is required to enable your salespeople to operate with meaningful sales forecasts and sales targets. It is also a key driver when you're planning the size and scope of your sales team.

Your goal is to arrive at an estimate of the realistic

market for your company's products. The process starts with the global market for a product – the Total Addressable Market (TAM) to which filters are added to account for the constraints on your company grabbing the entire market, giving you the Served Available Market (SAM). When you've allowed for the different factors that prevent you selling to the TAM, the number, whether in monetary or unit terms, should represent the sales your company could realistically secure and this becomes your Target Market (TM).

1. How big is the Total Addressable Market for your product?

The starting point is to estimate the TAM for your product, assuming that your company wins 100% market share.

- Start with an estimate of the national and global market for your product in both unit and value terms
- Estimate how fast the market for your product is growing, without that, it's impossible to tell whether market share is being won or lost and whether your salespeople are doing a good job

2. How big is the Served Available Market

The SAM is what is left after you've allowed for the constraints that prevent you serving the TAM. These factors might include:

- Size of your company
- Growth potential

- Geographic constraints:
    - Does the sale have to be completed face to face?
    - Do your staff need to be able to reach the customer physically?
    - Overseas sales – are cost, regulatory, tariff, technical or other factors limiting your export potential?

In reality, your company is unlikely to service the whole market but will have a segment. This will be driven by your budget and strategy.

3. How big is your Target Market?

You can use the information you've gathered to identify your target market, priority segments and key customers.

What is the size of your target market for each product?

You can use the same process for each product or service you offer. Estimate the annual reachable market for each product in total, then apply your constraints and you will reach an educated estimate in terms of sales and numbers of customers.

Which business sectors do your customers operate in?

The more information you have about your target customers, the more successful you will be in refining your sales and marketing to reach them.

Consider the following:

- Are your customers in a single industry or across several different sectors?
- Do your customers cover an entire market segment?
- In which specific business sector/activity do your customers operate?

Draw up a list of the sectors into which your product is sold and the companies in those sectors, that fall into the targeted geographic area. Using historic sales figures, estimate your company's current market share.

Which customers are you most likely to sell to?

- Identify and quantify customers you can sell to, define your ideal customer – the person most likely to buy from you
- Which customers have the most pressing problems or the highest priority needs that your product can solve?
- Which customers are most likely to respond to your brand proposition?

Apply subjective criteria to identify customers most likely to respond to your value proposition.

How big is your typical customer?

Identify those who meet the size criteria for purchasing and filter out those who do not.

- How much does your typical customer spend on your product?

- What is the annual revenue of your typical customer?
- Is your product aimed at small, medium or large businesses or could it be sold to any size business?
- Does the price of your product prohibit some companies from buying it; do they need to be a certain size to buy it? (e.g. you won't sell a £10m solution to a £1m annual revenue business)

Using all the information you have as a starting point, you can create a detailed list of target companies, prioritising the ones you estimate have the greatest potential. Consider whether the addressable market could be significantly increased with changes to your product or service offering - assuming that any changes are economically and technically viable.

Competitive Landscape

When I first started selling life insurance I went through an induction course. It was in the very early days of computer based training and computer graphics were almost non-existent. There was a series of very chunky characters on the green and black screen, each with the name of our competitors on their chest. I could select each one and hit enter to reveal information about the company, their products and their sales tactics. It was pretty basic stuff.

The good news is we've advanced in technology and understand that we need to know what our competitors are doing. The bad news is that all too often businesses lack sales strategies to combat a competitive situation and worse still, there are those who don't acknowledge that there even are real competitive alternatives to their offering.

GOAL: *To gain a deeper understanding of your competitors and the market into which your company sells.*

DISCOVERY: *A structured analysis of the market for your products and the nature of your competitors.*

The market:

As part of the process of estimating the potential market size for your products and services it is advisable to understand the strength, strategy and volume of your competitors.
If you don't follow market developments closely you will be unprepared to take advantage of changes or deal

with threats. Key questions to answer are:

- How is your competitive landscape evolving and what is driving the change?
- What new developments – technological or otherwise – are occurring?
- Is the market declining, stagnant or expanding?
- How many competitors do you have and who are they?
- Are more companies entering the market?
-

Competitors – who are they, what are they like?

- What kinds of companies compete in your market?
- Is there a large dominant player or is the market highly fragmented with a lot of smaller players?
- How do companies usually compete within the market?
- Is it about product quality, level of service, price, innovation or strength of brand?
- Are your competitors typically: aggressive/new/hungry/passive/established/lazy?
- What do your specific competitors offer and how do they compete?

Competitors – how much do you know about them?

- How much do you know about your competitors?
- Have you taken the time to find out?
- Do you know that lack of knowledge makes it difficult to plan how to position your business to beat them?

You should undertake a formal analysis of your competition researching factors such as:

- Revenue
- Growth rates
- Business mix
- Sectors in which they compete
- Strengths
- Weaknesses
- Market perception
- Pricing
- Other competitive strategies

Do you have an information-gathering strategy?

You probably put a lot of material into the public domain and your competitors will do the same. This is a valuable resource for building a picture of your close competition. In addition, your customers will be a good source of information on your competitors.

Your salespeople are in direct contact with your customers and it is a natural fit for them to take on the role of information gatherers. You might consider including collecting competitor intelligence as a KPI, to ensure your salespeople understand how important it is and what an impact it can have on your company's success.

Once you have the information it should be shared with senior management and other departments such as product design and research, to ensure you are able to match any new developments.

In order to counter your competitors' place in the market,

you need to understand their strengths and weaknesses, and compare their offerings to your own products. You may be able to identify gaps in the market that would be easy to for to fill. For example, if your customers mentioned a general dissatisfaction with post-sales service, you could step up your own efforts in that area to create a new USP.

Do you regularly do the following?

- Analyse your competitors' websites

- Follow their social media to see how they engage with their customers?

- Talk to your own customers about your competitors?

- Ask your customers why they choose to buy from you and not another supplier, ask them about your competitors strengths and weaknesses

- Get your salespeople to gather market and competitor information – provide the questions you want them to ask and make sure they understand what information you want

- Use the information your salespeople collect on the front-line to influence your strategic thinking, particularly the insights into any changes in pricing, demands for different types of products and their perceptions of any major market shifts or competitor movement

- Speak to your distributors, they are a link in the

chain between the manufacturer and the end-user and may have a valuable insight into your competitors

- Consider your competitors USPs and how they position their products

After the data has been collated, your salespeople should be able to use it in the field. If you have a regular channel for your salespeople to receive competitive information, they will understand the value of collecting and using it to achieve your company's objectives.

Sales Battlecard

A useful tool for your salespeople is the Battlecard. It is useful to create one for each of your major competitors. Similar to, but going beyond a SWOT analysis, the Battlecard is used to detail the relative strengths and weaknesses of your competitors' products, in addition to profiling their activities and market positioning in comparison to your offerings. The Battlecard will allow you to see how each of your competitors stack up against your product offerings in the market and will highlight ways in which they can be countered or exploited.

Sample Battlecard

Competitor Sales Battlecard

Their Product	Its Strengths	Its Weaknesses	Price Comparison
The product and services that they provide in total	Your perception of the competitor's areas of strength	Your perception of the competitor's areas of weakness	How your competitor's price compares to yours

Their Company	How they Position	Our Repositioning	Their Target Market
Detailed summary of the competitor, include how they operate, their routes to market and how long they've been established. Provide as much detail as possible	Provide an overview of the competitor's position in the market and how they differentiate against you and their other competition	How you propose to compete against them. How you could reposition your proposition against theirs. How you propose to differentiate your offering	Provide details of other areas in which your competitor operates and why that might make your proposition more focussed and relevant

Market Presence	Quick Tips	How to Win/Success	When to Walk Away
Up to date information about their company and their structure	Ways to demonstrate that you provide more value. Be aware, never knowingly knock the competition	Provide details of how you have won against the competitor before and give references and examples when possible	The competitor is likely to come back with a counter offer so be prepared to know your walk away point – discuss with your team/chain of command

Go To Market Strategy

On the trawler we had a strict hierarchy and I was on the very bottom rung. I was 16 years old and straight out of school, I didn't know very much about anything at all. I was told what to do and when to do it and I didn't question it, but it wasn't long before I started to analyse what we did and why and when it changed. The skipper was an experienced old hand and knew exactly which fish were in season and exactly when and where they'd be. He'd issue orders according to his plan and we'd load the boat. A bottom trawl meant mixed fishing. Trammel nets for sole, scallop dredges for scallops and lobster pots for lobsters. Different equipment, different tactics for different products – in this case fish. It was a successful boat and my first lesson in a go to market strategy.

GOAL: *To create an action plan for delivering your product or service.*

DISCOVERY: *Does your company have a clear plan for bringing products to market and are the routes you've chosen the best and most appropriate?*

A go to market strategy is an action plan that shows how you will reach your customers and create a competitive advantage. It covers a number of areas, but basically answers four questions:

- What are you selling?
- Who are you selling to?
- How will you reach your target market?
- How will you promote your product?

Define the offer: What are you selling?

- What is your value proposition and the main business benefit for your customer?
- What problem is being solved?
- What are the main benefits of your product?
- How will your product be used?
- How is your product different from your competitors' offerings?

Define target market: Who are you selling to?

- Who would you expect to buy your product?
- Define the profile of your typical customer.

Sales channels and marketing strategy: How will you reach your target market?

- What are your predominant marketing channels?
- Do they match your products and the way your customers prefer to interact with your business?
- Do you have a clear idea of where your customers go to buy products in the market segment?
- Do the channels and the way your products are sold through them, leverage your value proposition?
- If your value proposition is about quality, price, service etc. is that evident in the channel strategy?
- Do your current channels allow access to the addressable market and the highest priority customers within it?
- Are there under-exploited channels e.g. should

you be getting more direct referrals from existing customers?

- Do you have strategic partnerships?

Branding, marketing and pricing: How will you promote your product?

- Does your selling approach reflect your brand positioning?
- Does your brand message come through clearly in each channel?
- Have you included the insights from your competitive landscape analysis?
- Are your competitors' relative strengths in different product areas being countered effectively?

ACTIONS:

- Analyse your previous sales sources to determine where the majority of your sales have come from historically and which sources provided the largest or most profitable customers
- Customer profile - profile the characteristics of your best customers. Translate that profile into a 'buyer persona' to create a picture of your ideal customer
- Conduct a branding review and include your own and your competitors' offerings for comparison
- Define your offer - determine who will use your product and how, what are the major benefits and how your product is different
- Analyse your sales and marketing materials to check they are making the most of your competitive strengths

- List all your marketing collateral including: website, online content (white papers, case studies for inbound marketing), leaflets and other print collateral, does it properly represent your product offering and branding?

- How does your pricing stack up against your competition and does it equate to the value delivered by your product?

- Have you considered which channel is the optimum way to reach your customers and is that channel available and fully developed?

- Is your sales process set up to maximise the amount of business coming through your chosen channel?

- The value proposition should drive your strategy; does your GTM strategy reflect your competitive analysis?

- Analyse all your marketing channels and determine whether they match the value proposition e.g. high value products/services or those requiring a high degree of human interaction should not be sold via a website which is, in effect, self-serve

- How do you identify your prospects, market to them, bid for their business and win their custom - is your process consistent and repeatable?

- Have you measured the effectiveness of each sales channel to understand which needs more attention, either because it's working well or because it's not working?

- Do you know the return on investment for each sales channel?

- Do you have a formal, written GTM Strategy for each product segment?

- Establish a formal process for measuring the success or failure of each sales channel

Included in your Go To Market Strategy should be:

- Strategic objectives
- Resources required for implementation
- Budget
- Timeline
- Measurement of success

It is vital to keep communicating to your staff until you're confident that every person in your business is able to say 'This is where we're going and this is how we're going to get there.'

People

Building a sustainable team is about identifying and training the best people for the job. Dealing with your people is challenging and can be exciting, frustrating and, of course, costs you time and money.

Finding and keeping a team needs constant work. The revolving door of sales staff destabilises your team and affects your whole company through lost sales growth and morale. It can happen if there is a tendency to quick hire and fire, caused by an inadequate process for hiring and onboarding in the people space.

It is one of the biggest challenges faced by business owners, the one guaranteed to keep you up at night. It may be hard to find and hire the right staff, but when you have a consistent process it becomes easier. You have steps, you follow them and you know you're doing the right thing. If after all that, you still have a disastrous hire and need to fire, you will be able to see at which point the person didn't meet your expectations and you will know it was not a failing of your due diligence. What's more, morale and productivity are less likely to be damaged because your existing team will be able to see that a fair and equitable process was followed.

Once you've selected your staff, know their skill sets, have mapped their capabilities, strengths and potential and have set up their thorough onboarding plan, you're ready to set them loose on your customers.

A good team and how it works needs regular assessment and review. Training and mentoring for your teams and individuals is vital to keep them at the top of their game.

How to motivate a team of individuals can be difficult but financial reward and recognition are always effective. Developing good incentives, a fair commission and compensation structure and bonus plans, will ensure you reward your great performers and encourage all the team to achieve their best.

People are perhaps your most valuable asset and how you train and develop them, how you treat them and how you reward them, affects both your growth and profit and the perception of your company in the competitive market.

Vision	People	Process	Management
Alignment to Corporate Strategy	**Roles and Responsibility**	Sales and Marketing Alignment	Forecasting Metrics and KPIs
Value Proposition	**Hiring and Onboarding**	Methodology and Winning Customers	Sales Meetings and Structures
Addressable Market	**Training and Development**	Maximising Lifetime Value	Performance Management
Competitive Landscape	**Salary Commission and Bonuses**	CRM and Technology	Strategic Sales Planning
Go To Market Strategy	**Culture and Knowledge Sharing**	Documentation and Collateral	Integration with the Wider Business

The five key elements are:

Sales Roles and Responsibilities
- Are there different levels of sales staff with varying responsibilities and how do they operate?

Hiring and Onboarding
- Is there a strategy for recruiting new sales staff and a process for onboarding them?

Training and Development
- Are there training programmes and education for sales staff with the opportunity for development and promotion?

Salary, Commission and Bonus Schemes
- How do your commission and bonus schemes work and does your remuneration process have a positive effect on the behaviour of your sales department, encouraging them to achieve your company's objectives?

Culture and Knowledge Sharing
- Can you describe your company's culture and is there a robust process for gathering, documenting and knowledge sharing?

Sales Roles and Responsibilities

I'm absolutely rubbish at any form of DIY. If the level of skill required to complete a certain task is beyond hammering in a nail, I'm pretty much done for. I don't sweat this stuff though because I reckon if you need to build a garden wall you hire a bricklayer; if you want a tree house you get a carpenter and if your sink's leaking, you get a plumber. It is possible to find an odd job person who's able to cover all these and they might even be good, but they won't be as good as a specialist – the key is the right person for the job.

GOAL: *To investigate whether your company understands who does what and why in your sales function.*

DISCOVERY: *How does your company stack up against the sales team model?*

There are many different roles in a sales team. What you have will depend on the size and needs of your company, the industry in which you operate, your customers, how they buy and numerous other factors. You may have many different, often overlapping, roles within your business.

The more junior sales roles are usually engaged with the initial stages of the sales process. The more senior roles will focus on the later stages, as the stakes get higher, because significant time and money may have been invested in winning the business. The sales person responsible for longer term strategic planning, as well as team management, is usually in at the close but again this will depend on your business and how you sell to your customers.

For this example of a sales team, I have picked six sales roles and their main functions:

- **The Telemarketer**: *Focus on lead generation -* office based
  The Telemarketer will develop prospect lists, make sales calls and book sales appointments

- **The Internal Sales Person**: *Focus on both lead generation and conversion -* office based
  The Internal Sales Person will carry out the same activities the Telemarketer and will create proposals for customers, negotiate prices and close sales

- **The Sales Executive**: *Focus on both lead generation and conversion -* field based
  The Sales Executive will perform the same activities as the Internal Sales Person and will attend sales meetings with customers

- **The Key Accounts Manager:** *Focus on conversion -* field based
  The Key Accounts Manager will perform the same duties as the Sales Executive but they will not generate leads. Instead, they are responsible for the growth and sales activity of designated priority accounts

- **The Sales Manager:** *Focus on conversion plus managerial responsibilities -* office and field based

The Sales Manager's main function is to manage and develop the sales team. They are responsible for coaching, training and sales plan implementation.

- **The Sales Director:** *Focus on some key elements of conversion plus strategy* – office and field based
  The Sales Director has some overlap with the Sales Manager, but they have the additional responsibility for developing the overall business sales strategy and accountability for achieving the company sales targets.

These six sample roles in the sales process require individuals with specific skills and experience if they are to be successful in the different roles. This will be the case with any sales roles you need in your company. You should not expect one salesperson to do everything or to be able to do everything. It is unlikely that one person would have the appropriate skills to manage lead creation, meeting initiation, making presentations, negotiating terms, coaching and training, creating strategy and closing the deal. Each sales role requires a different skill-set and, particularly in the senior roles, significant experience.

ACTION:

- If you had no sales staff, for which functions would you need to hire people?

- How does your current sales structure compare to the outline of the six sample sales roles and what roles do you think you need to suit your business?

- Are the roles within your sales function as clearly defined as they should be?

- Is there 'mission creep' with some sales staff expected to cover more functions than their role requires?

- When you consider the six sample sales roles outlined here for demonstration purposes, do any of your current employees sit in one of these?

- Are you 100% clear on what it is you actually want people to do when you're recruiting sales staff?

- Have you identified the specific roles you want people to fill or do you hope that you will find people whose skills can overlap?

- Think about the appropriate sales structure for your products/services and remember, there is a huge variety of sales roles, and they can and will vary significantly depending on the type of business you have. If you think your product or service requires a more customised approach, how would you reflect that in your sales structure?

Put together a Sales Responsibility Matrix, AKA 'Who is doing what in your sales department?' This will help you clarify exactly what is expected of each sales person in the team. It's a useful exercise to get you thinking about what you're expecting of your sales staff and whether they're able to achieve it.

Hiring and Onboarding

I bumped into the sister of a local guy who used to work for me; actually I'd given him his first job in sales. We chatted for a minute or two and then I had to ask: 'How's your brother doing these days?' She grinned. 'Oh he's working in London for an investment company.' He was a really likeable character and I was happy to hear that he seemed to be doing well. She looked proud as punch and continued: 'Yes, he's one of their top performers and he's just bought a million-pound house in Kent.'

When I hired him, the guy in question knew nothing about sales. I failed to spend enough time with him, failed to give him the training he needed and failed to set him up to be successful in my company, so he moved on. The loss was mine.

Goal: *To investigate whether your hiring strategy is underpinned by a clear plan and whether your onboarding process sets your new sales people up for success.*

Discovery: *How have you recruited staff in the past, do you have a structured process and what happens right after you hire them?*

There are three important parts to the process of hiring new employees and bringing them on board:

1. Definition of roles and skills required

Start with a clear definition of the different roles in your sales team. The main elements of the sales process are building leads, converting them, after sale management and directing sales at a strategic level. You will need a full job description for each role you want to fill, outlining the responsibilities and identifying the key skills required. This will allow you to recruit with a clear idea of the skills and experience you're looking for.

2. A clear recruitment strategy

There are two approaches to finding the ideal candidate to fill your role:

Build - develop a young inexperienced person who can undertake structured training to obtain the skills, learn how to use the tools and processes that underpin a good sales programme.

Advantages	Disadvantages
Cheaper to hire	Length of time it takes to train
Train and develop desirable skills	Structured training programme will be needed
Mentor good attitude and behaviour	Impact on your sales team supporting less effective trainee
Potential for long term growth and promotion	Long term return on investment - will not have immediate an impact on your sales growth

Buy - appoint an experienced sales person in your industry who will hit the ground running and may bring their own sales book of contacts to the benefit of your company

Advantages	Disadvantages
Quick to achieve sales growth – quick return on investment	High salary and bonus commensurate with experience
Industry experience and contacts	Expectation of infrastructure and processes to match or exceed previous employment
Confidence and experience will generate confidence in customers	Long term uncertainty
May bring new customers to your company	Likely expectation of salary increase upon results before you're ready to afford it
	Impact on your sales team accepting expensive high flyer

Both approaches can work but there are pitfalls to hiring people just because they have industry experience or a great 'black book'. Seeking specific experience within your industry, products and type of customers, seems logical but can lead to hiring job-hoppers. 10 years of industry experience may sound impressive, but it can mean the person has consistently failed. The 10 years could be one year of experience, repeated ten times, in ten different companies. A talented, process-oriented sales person will be able to learn your industry and products.

If you do hire a maverick 'star' you'll have committed a substantial amount of investment if it doesn't work out. Hiring people who are process driven, with the skills, habits and behaviour you want is a safer option. Sales people with the right attitude will be able to learn the specifics of your products and services and the differences in the sales process in your industry. A positive attitude and plenty of energy trumps everything. Hire attitude and you will be able to train the sales skills you need.

3. Implementation of a structured onboarding process for your new staff

Do you expect your new sales person to fit in and learn the ropes on their first day? If you assume your new sales person will be able to start selling the minute they set foot in the door you are setting them up to fail. You can't just expect them to know what's required of them, you must tell them. If you provide a structured programme that covers all the key areas of your business, products and industry you will be rewarded quickly because you have set them up to succeed. Not only that, you have demonstrated that you support and value them.

ACTIONS:

Hiring

- Create standard job descriptions for each role within your sales process, listing the skills and personality traits required for each role

- Think about your main source for new employees – have you primarily hired experienced industry people or have you relied on training younger recruits?

- Analyse your previous hires and assess how successful employees from each source have been

- Review your current recruitment process. Do you have a structured approach to selecting, interviewing and vetting candidates?

- If you don't have a structure, create one

- Establish a set of skill-based questions to use when you interview your candidates

- If you are looking at more experienced salespeople, don't skimp on your due diligence. Candidates can be creative with the truth about why they left their last job and what their experience actually is. Don't accept simple answers, dig in and ask more questions and do your own research

- Hire slowly, but if it's not working, fire quickly.

You should always be looking to hire talent, even if you have no gap when an opportunity presents itself. Waiting until your situation is urgent can lead to bad decisions. If you find yourself behind on your numbers you might rush into hiring somebody for the short term who can hit the ground running and give you the boost you need. This strategy is costly and rarely works. Planning ahead, always being on the lookout for talent, will allow you to create a stable and well performing sales team.

Onboarding

- If you don't have one, develop a structured onboarding programme. New staff need to understand the company vision, the value to the clients of the products, the sales methodology specific to your product/service, the nature of your competitors and how their performance will be evaluated

- At the end of the onboarding programme, your new employee should understand the company goals and their own role in helping to achieve them

- Any training and practice elements (e.g. role-playing) that you build into your onboarding programme should be continued beyond the induction process

Create a sales onboarding plan for the induction and mobilisation of a new sales recruit, which will then act as a checklist, if they fail to perform to your expectations and requirements.

Your onboarding plan should be at a granular level focussing on days 1-7 to start, laying out weeks 1-4 and then months 1-6. If you take this approach, with expectations, goals and objectives clearly set out, your new employee will be able to transition smoothly into your company. At any stage you will be able to analyse how they are fitting in, whether they are meeting your expectations and take any remedial action required.

Sample Onboarding Plan for a New Sales Recruit

Sample Sections	Day 1	Week 1	Month 1	Month 2-3	Month 4-6
Company	Understand company history Its values and beliefs, Introduced to your 'buddy'	Lunch with 'buddy', Lunch with Line Manager	Be able to recite the story of your company, Position the 'elevator pitch'	Understand the operational workings of your business	Deliver a full presentation to a new prospect
Sectors	Understand your markets, Who you sell to and why	Marquee client's names, How and why they choose you	Working knowledge of the market in which you operate, Understand why marquee clients buy from you, The value you add to the market	Keeping abreast of the major industry developments	Become knowledgeable in the sector and able to share knowledge
Products	Your product positioning, Where you sit in the market	Understand your competitive landscape, Learn how you differentiate	Comprehensive understanding of your product portfolio, Know how you stack up compared to your competition	Ability to present and communicate product or service value and benefits	Independent and able to conduct quality meetings (internally and externally)
Process	Read the Sales Playbook, Get 'buddy' to share customer journey	Understand how you win, Understand what not to do	Confident with key sales processes	Proficient in customer engagement aligned to process	Be able to articulate the full customer journey, Demonstrate best practice of the entire sales process, Be able to on board another recruit
Tools (Sales Aids)	Study website, Read Case Studies	Read Fact Sheets, Read Battlecards, Watch relevant videos	Proficient in all internal sales workings (CRM and reporting)	Able to generate clear and compelling proposals	Full understanding of the entire company literature
Sales Activity	Shadow successful people, Discuss your sales plan with your Line Manager	Observe prospecting and sales activities, Complete sales plan	Complete and pass first sales training sessions, Observe a live sales pitch, Complete sales plan, Start developing prospect pipeline	Continue to develop own pipeline and negotiate first wins, Attend first own sales calls	Quality pipeline and regularly winning business, Make regular contribution to the wider business

Example Job Descriptions for Sales Staff

When creating your job descriptions, the key responsibilities outline the exact tasks the successful candidate will work on, and it helps to break the skill and experience into 'essential' and 'nice to have'. This gives you flexibility to hire for attitude, while at the same time ensuring your candidate already has the basic skills and experience you need. I have included example job descriptions for the sample sales team we looked at in the section: 'Sales Roles and Responsibilities.

Sales roles are numerous and often unique to a company or specific product. You might decide to define a role that suits your company with a combination of factors from different roles. As long as you are clear in your job description, you have flexibility to create the roles you need.

This flexibility can add to the difficulty when you're looking to hire good staff with experience. If an otherwise good candidate doesn't have something on your essential list, remember you put it there for a good reason. It's important not to be swayed by recommendations, because experience in another company may not transferable to yours if you have unique and specific requirements.

Telemarketer

To succeed in this role you will need to be a motivated Telemarketer responsible for and able to generate leads proactively and in a confident manner, assist new and existing customers and achieve individual and company targets. You must have previous experience in Telemarketing within the industry sector.

Key Responsibilities

- As part of the team, you will draw on your ability to have good quality conversations when speaking with new and existing customers
- Manage inbound calls from our new and existing customers by providing exceptional customer service and sales skills
- Create a connection with your customer by understanding their needs
- Up sell and cross sell products by promoting the benefits to customers
- Drive for results and work towards targets
- Demonstrate the company's values and behaviour

Essential Skills & Experience

- The ability to work in a fast-paced, team-focused environment
- Strong customer focus and ability to connect with customers
- A proactive approach and resilience to overcome customer objections
- An aptitude for sales
- Experience working towards targets
- The ability to multi task and confidently manage multiple technologies
- Lead generation through proactive research and prequalification
- Able to work closely with the sales and marketing team

- The ability to converse easily with people at all levels in the organisation
- The ability to obtain information about companies and record findings in the CRM database

The successful candidate will possess the following:

- Previous experience in B2B Telemarketing/Telesales
- Business acumen and knowledge of business processes
- Professional telephone manner, excellent communication skills and a friendly manner
- Good attention to detail and an investigative nature
- Self motivation with high levels of energy and drive
- Confidence and lots of common sense
- Results focus with the ability to work to targets
- Patience and professionalism at all times

Example Job Description: Internal Sales Person

To succeed in this role you will need to be a motivated Sales Person responsible for and able to generate leads proactively and in a confident manner by phone. You will assist new and existing customers and achieve individual and company targets. You will also create proposals for customers, negotiate prices and close sales. You must have previous experience in all aspects of telephone-based sales within the industry sector

Key Responsibilities:

- As part of the team, you will draw on your ability to have good quality conversations when speaking with new and existing customers
- Manage inbound calls from our new and existing customers by providing exceptional customer service and sales skills
- Create a connection with your customer by understanding their needs
- Up sell and cross sell products by promoting the benefits to customers
- Create proposals, negotiate prices and close sales
- Drive for results and work towards targets
- Demonstrate the company's values and behaviour

Essential Skills and Experience:

- The ability to work in a fast-paced, team-focused environment
- Strong customer focus and ability to connect with customers

- A proactive approach and resilience to overcome customer objections
- An aptitude for sales
- Experience working towards targets
- The ability to multi task and confidently manage multiple technologies
- Lead generation through proactive research and prequalification
- Demonstrated ability to create proposals, negotiate prices and close sales
- Able to work closely with the sales and marketing team
- The ability to converse easily with people at all levels in the organisation
- The ability to obtain information about companies and record findings in the CRM database

The Successful Candidate will possess the following:

- Previous experience in B2B Telemarketing/Telesales
- Business acumen and knowledge of business processes
- At least two years' experience in creating proposals and closing sales
- Ability to understand and follow company process when negotiating prices
- Professional telephone manner, excellent communication skills and a friendly manner
- Good attention to detail and an investigative nature
- Self motivation with high levels of energy and drive

- Confidence and lots of common sense
- Results focus with the ability to work to targets
- Patience and professionalism at all times

Example Job Description: Sales Executive

To succeed in this role you will need to be a motivated Sales Person responsible for and able to generate leads proactively confidently both by phone and other appropriate methods. You will have a minimum of three years' experience in a sales role and will assist new and existing customers to achieve individual and company targets. You will be experienced in creating proposals, negotiating prices and closing sales. You will attend sales meetings with customers and must be comfortable with all levels of management. You must have previous experience in sales within the industry sector

Key Responsibilities:

- Manage customer inquiries
- Work to deadlines set by clients and the sales team
- Update and maintain the company administration systems
- Maximise sales opportunities
- Communicate effectively and in a timely manner to managers, supervisors, customers, suppliers and other departments
- Present to customers, create proposals, negotiate prices and close sales
- Up sell and cross sell products by promoting the benefits to customers
- Drive for results and work towards targets
- Demonstrate the company's values and behaviour

Essential skills and experience

- Three years' minimum successful track record in a business sales environment
- Excellent communication skills both written and verbal
- Self diary management and appointment booking
- The ability to work in a fast-paced, team-focused environment
- Strong customer focus and ability to connect with customers
- A proactive approach and resilience to overcome customer objections
- Experience working towards targets
- The ability to multi task and confidently manage multiple technologies
- Lead generation through proactive research and prequalification
- Demonstrated ability to create proposals, negotiate prices and close sales
- Able to work closely with the sales and marketing team
- The ability to converse easily with people at all levels in the organisation
- The ability to obtain information about companies and record findings in the CRM database
- Confident presentation skills
- Superior ability to work in a team

The Successful Candidate will possess the following:

- Minimum of three years' experience in a similar sales role
- Full clean United Kingdom driving license
- Professional, reliable and flexible attitude

- Have GCSE grade C and above in Maths and English
- Smart appearance
- Business acumen and knowledge of business processes
- Ability to understand and follow company process when negotiating prices
- Professional and courteous manner
- Good attention to detail and an investigative nature
- Self motivation with high levels of energy and drive
- Confidence and lots of common sense
- Results focus with the ability to work to targets
- Patience and professionalism at all times

Example Job Description: Key Accounts Manager

To succeed in this role you will need to be an experienced and motivated Sales Person. You will have a minimum of two years' experience in an account management role and be responsible for the growth and sales activity of designated priority accounts. You will oversee these existing relationships with the company's most important clients and be responsible for maintaining long-term key customers by understanding their requirements.
You will be adept in building strong relationships with strategic customers and able to identify their needs and requirements to promote the company's solutions while sustaining and growing the business to achieve long-term success.

Key Responsibilities:

- Develop trusted relationships with a portfolio of major clients to ensure they are retained
- Acquire a thorough understanding of key customer needs and requirements
- Expand the relationships with existing customers by proposing solutions that meet their objectives
- Ensure the correct products and services are delivered to key customers in a timely manner
- Serve as the link of communication between key customers and internal teams
- Resolve any issues and problems faced by key customers and deal with complaints to maintain trust
- Play an integral part in generating new sales with the view to creating long-lasting relationships

- Prepare regular reports of progress and forecasts to internal and external stakeholders using key account metrics

Essential skills and experience

- Proven experience as a key account manager
- BSc/BA in business administration, sales or relevant field
- Experience in sales and providing solutions based on customer needs
- Strong communication and interpersonal skills with an aptitude for building relationships with professionals at all organisational levels
- Excellent organisational skills
- Superior negotiation skills and proven ability to solve problems
- Excellent communication skills both written and verbal
- Self diary management and appointment booking
- Strong customer focus and ability to connect with customers
- A proactive approach and resilience to overcome customer objections
- Confident presentation skills
- Superior ability to work in a team

The Successful Candidate will possess the following:

- Proven experience in a similar sales role
- Full clean United Kingdom driving license

- Professional, reliable and flexible attitude
- Smart appearance
- Business acumen and knowledge of business processes
- Ability to understand and follow company process when negotiating prices
- Professional and courteous manner
- Good attention to detail and an investigative nature
- Self motivation with high levels of energy and drive
- Confidence and lots of common sense
- Results focus with the ability to work to targets
- Patience and professionalism at all times

Example Job Description: Sales Manager

To succeed in this role you will need to be a motivated and experienced Sales Leader. You will be responsible for the planning and review of departmental activities to process and maintain profitable expansion and ensure that excellent customer service is delivered. You will be expected to oversee the quality of service offered to customers, monitor the use of resources and control these against set budgets, ensure your staff are competent and sufficiently trained, make effective decisions which benefit the company, work smoothly alongside staff and your customer base and implement the strategic management and execution of sales. Previous experience in sales within the industry sector is desirable.

Key Responsibilities:

- Managing a team of Field Sales, Telesales and Account Managers
- Coaching, training and driving the sales function including shadowing some external client meetings
- Mentoring sales staff
- Setting revenue and performance targets
- Individual appraisals and one-to-one coaching and development
- Close working with other departments to develop special offers and lead generation
- Budget management and P&L

Essential skills and experience

- Previous sales management experience
- A natural leader with demonstrated results
- Proven sales experience and track record
- Be disciplined, fair, and resourceful to overcome any team difficulties
- Communicate effectively, easily and in a timely manner to all company management and staff
- Confident presentation skills
- Self-motivation with integrity and the ability to remain calm under pressure
- Superior leadership skills
- Strong customer focus and ability to connect with customers and sales team

The Successful Candidate will possess the following:

- Demonstrated experience in a similar sales leadership role
- Full clean United Kingdom driving license
- Professional, reliable and flexible attitude
- Smart appearance
- Business acumen and knowledge of business processes
- Professional and courteous manner
- Good attention to detail and an investigative nature
- Self motivation with high levels of energy and drive
- Results focus with the ability to work to targets
- Patience and professionalism at all times

Example Job Description: Sales Director

To succeed in this role you will need to be a motivated and experienced Sales Leader. You will be responsible for the development of the overall business sales strategy and for delivering the total sales targets. You will be accountable for the performance of the sales leadership team and will be required to present to senior management and the board. You will demonstrate a high level of interpersonal skills with the ability to communicate and manage well at all levels. Previous experience in sales within the industry sector is desirable.

Key Responsibilities:

- Responsible for the performance of the sales leadership team
- Primary accountability for the day to day leadership of all aspects of sales growth
- Be instrumental in leading the sales activity to drive sales
- Oversee all sales channels and sales functions
- Drive growth by achieving optimum operational performance
- Ensure that sales, financial, commercial and operational best practice is followed to achieve revenue growth

Essential skills and experience:

- Minimum ten years' B2B sales experience
- Minimum five years' experience in sales and business management
- Demonstrated success in sales growth
- Demonstrated experience in the building and successful management of sales teams

- Superior leadership skills and team building competence
- High level of interpersonal skills with the ability to communicate to all levels in the organisation
- Deadline focused, well organised with sound judgement

The Successful Candidate will possess the following:

- Demonstrated experience in a similar sales leadership role
- Able to take direction and execute strategy
- Able to exercise sound judgement and make decisions based on accurate and timely analyses
- Possess a proven track record of personal, academic and professional achievements
- Strong business orientation and commercial acumen
- Advanced user of Microsoft office and other relevant software
- Full clean United Kingdom driving license
- Professional, reliable and flexible attitude
- Smart appearance
- Patience and professionalism at all times
- Knowledge of and adherence to all health and safety practices

If you read through all the job descriptions in this example, you will be able to see a clear road to promotion from Telemarketer through to Sales Director. It is important to ensure that all your staff, new and existing, know about opportunities for promotion. Awareness of the next step for an employee can be a powerful motivator and if they are able to see how it can be achieved, it will work as a solid retention tool for your best staff.

Training and Development

Having been a 16-year-old working on a trawler, the saying 'Give a man a fish and you feed him for a day; teach a man to fish and you feed him for a lifetime' always resonates with me. I was the most junior in the crew of three and my 'training' was just watching the others and doing what they did, the best I could. At that age I didn't expect anything else, didn't really even think about it, but I did realise early on that I wasn't going to do the job for long. I don't know if it was the lack of training that made me think that or an understanding that I wanted more and was capable of much more. Some years later, I jumped at the chance to sign up to sell Life Insurance on a commission only basis. Not because I had any desire to flog Life Insurance, but because they offered excellent sales training. I knew that with good training I'd have skills for life.

Goal: *To investigate whether training and development is an integral part of your operation.*

Discovery: *How well developed are your training functions?*

Training and Development are related but have distinctive characteristics.

- Training – specific skills that are usually related to your products and directly to the role of the trainee
- Development - general transferable skills for the personal development the individual trainee not related to your products

Training

Structured sales training should be undertaken on a regular basis. It's a mistake to think it isn't important. Don't listen to people who want to just 'wing it'. If you're serious about building a sustainable sales team, you need to focus time, effort and resources on systems and processes. If your sales people aren't getting their knowledge in a structured sales training situation, they will learn and practice sales skills on the job in front of prospects, which could result in losing valuable leads. This is not a desirable scenario leading to lost revenue and damage to the reputation of your company.

Sales is a structured process and the skills have to be learned. When they are learned, they should be practiced and updated to ensure bad habits, short cuts and poor time management haven't eroded the skill base. Salespeople should not be allowed to use live customers as a training tool and only a structured sales training regime will prevent this.

Good training starts from the moment a new employee joins your company. A structured onboarding is the best way to ensure you are building a culture that values regular sales training.

The type of training you undertake will vary according to your industry and its requirements. Whatever your requirements are, you should think about what you want your sales staff to achieve and how they will achieve it.

The most effective training identifies the components in the sales function and trains for these as individual parts of the sale. They might include:

- The meet and greet
- Role-playing the presentation and pitch
- Rehearsing negotiation
- The close

In addition to these are personal skills. They might include:

- How you conduct the meeting
- Listening rather than talking
- Client questions and probing for more detail

Personal skills can be deemed 'soft' but are of equal importance to 'hard' sales skills.

Development

If training is about learning specific product and job-related skills, development is a longer-term process for the benefit of the individual. Training is usually delivered in groups with a standardised curriculum and with set outcomes required. Development is personal, conducted one on one with an individual.

In practice, it can mean offering your employees the option to undertake certification programmes to gain additional qualifications. While these can help in their current role, it also benefits them personally, preparing them for future career development. Development can also include formal mentoring and coaching with more experienced colleagues.

It is important to have an ongoing plan for your employees to demonstrate how they will be able to progress within your business. Personal and career development, a vision of how their skills and knowledge will be nurtured, is important to employees. An effective plan can play a big part in retaining your best talent.

Training and development are central to the success of your businesses. Growing and developing the talent you have, is a better long-term strategy than trying to buy it in. When you recruit new staff, look for people who are willing to be trained. Anyone who says they don't want or need training and development is waving a giant red flag.

ACTIONS:

Conduct a training and development audit of your business:

- Is training a regular fixture in your sales staff timetable?
- If it isn't, when was the last time you offered a sales training session?
- Do your salespeople know that they will required to learn, refresh and practice their skills on a regular basis?
- Do they understand where individual training sessions fit in to the bigger picture related to their day-to-day roles and to your company's goals?
- Do you have someone in your organisation with the responsibility to drive the training programme?
- Are your managers aware of their teams' training and development needs?

- Are your salespeople sceptical and resistant towards training?

Planning Training and Development

The specifics of training and development take many forms and will vary from business to business but there are consistent underlying principles:

- Training should take place at regular, consistent times with consistent content
- Remove staff from their familiar environment to engage in role-playing. This allows sales staff to learn to deal with unexpected situations, customer questions and objections
- Training should cover three basic areas:
  o Generic sales training - skills applicable to selling in general
  o Product training - covering specific company offerings
  o Presentation training - showing real-life examples of successful techniques and allowing salespeople to practice in a low risk environment
- Break the sales process down into its component parts to make it modular
- Deliver it in digestible chunks, allowing specific parts to be regularly revisited
- Use the company's most valuable asset: its best people, to mentor new sales staff
- Provide refreshers for experienced salespeople to update them on the company's products, the specific value proposition and the competitive landscape

Salary, Commission and Bonus Schemes

As I've considered the different sections of this book, I've realised how much I learned about life from my time on the trawler. I don't know whether it's something to do with the sheer physicality and drudgery of the work, but it taught me a lot.

Income for everyone on the boat was based on a share of the catch so it was either feast or famine. I was on a government initiative aimed at keeping school leavers off the dole. It was called the Youth Training Scheme; it was a fixed rate allowance of not quite 28 quid, rising to 35, if I made it to a second year. The skipper paid me the allowance in cash at the end of every week and as you can imagine, it was hard to survive on so little, especially on a week of good catches when I knew how much the boat was making.

The crew's share of the catch was based on percentage. After expenses were accounted for, usually half the profit, the skipper took 5/9ths, the crewman took 3/9ths and I, lowest of the low, got 1/9th on top of my 28 quid from the government. I never got more than 20 quid.

I remember one time, for about a week, the fish were so plentiful that we doubled and trebled our usual catch every time we went out. As luck would have it, it was just the skipper and me working, as our other crewmember was having a week's holiday in the West Country. I worked my heart out hauling the nets in, gutting the fish, doing three or four times my usual workload for my pitiful training allowance. Our absent crew member heard about the huge catches we were making and came back early to work the last two days of this unusual week. He couldn't afford to miss out because he knew his share for two days, would be more than he earned in a normal week. At last payday came and the skipper congratulated me, said how much he appreciated my efforts and handed over my 28 quid. I knew he'd given the other guy a few hundred pounds for the two days he'd worked, so I had great expectations. After all, I'd done the bulk of the work every day, so when he solemnly handed over a 20-pound note, I felt shattered. 20 quid didn't even come close to being 1/9th of what the catch had made. I calculated that I'd worked a seven-day week at 16 hours a day. That's over a 100 solid hours of hauling nets, gutting, washing and boxing fish. I was expecting about 100 quid and I felt as gutted as the fish. I learned a very good and very tough lesson that day.

Goal: *To investigate whether your remuneration scheme encourages the right behaviour.*

Discovery: *What combination of salary, commission and bonus schemes are you using and are they achieving your business goals?*

To achieve an effective remuneration structure, it is important to understand how the balance between salary, commission and bonuses, drives the behaviour of your staff. If you approach remuneration from benchmarking the market rate, you are not including incentives to encourage the behaviour you want to see in your sales people. Decide where your company is currently sitting and what goals and objectives you have set.

- Are looking to expand your market share aggressively by grabbing as much new business as possible?
    - If you are, your salespeople might be incentivised on the volume of new orders

- Is your goal to increase the average order size?
    - If you are, the performance of your salespeople will be assessed on the overall change in order size achieved

- Do you want to boost margins, even at the short-term expense of sales growth?
    - If you do, the incentive would not be linked to total sales volumes but to the overall profit margin on the sales

The remuneration structure must be aligned with your corporate goals – literally paying your people to achieve what you want. Each of the examples above requires a different remuneration strategy. If your priority is higher margins rather than raw sales growth, you wouldn't remunerate your salespeople to reward them for 'shift the product at any price' behaviour. You wouldn't get their best effort and they wouldn't be content with their pay.

Salary, commission and bonus schemes are there to prompt the right activities in a broader sense as well. Having the wrong blend can trigger undesirable behaviour. A low base salary could encourage your salespeople to push to close deals and earn commission even if it's wrong for the customer, damaging your company's reputation in the long term.

The remuneration structure also varies with the sales role. A job focused on winning new customers requires different characters – hunters, from a role managing and developing existing accounts – farmers/nurturers. These separate disciplines also demand different behaviour.

A lower salary coupled with high bonus levels would be appropriate for salespeople tasked with bringing in new business, opening new markets and accounts, and building something from nothing. Overpaying on base salary would remove the incentive for salespeople in these roles to go the extra mile to earn the extra money.

Conversely, salespeople maintaining and developing existing customers are likely to be steadier characters with an eye to the long term. They will need a good base salary with a more modest bonus. You already know their customer is going to be spending more money with your company and the sales person is rewarded for managing not creating.

It's easy to forget that it's not all about the money, even in a highly competitive sales environment, where financial rewards are highly valued. Non-financial motivators can be significant too and can include:

Brand – Belief in the brand and the product
Culture – A culture that that resonates with the individual is a huge incentive
Values & Leadership – Leaders who embody the culture, inspirational and leading by example
Impact – If the individual feels they can make an impact in a way they care about
Development – Opportunities to grow and develop new skills

Action:

Conduct a remuneration audit on your company:

- How are your remuneration decisions made, do they reflect the perceived going rate or do they take account of your company's goals?
- Are your company's goals – sales growth, margin expansion, opening up new markets, aligned to your remuneration policies?
- How many different remuneration structures do you have in your business?
- Does the balance between salary/commission/bonus reflect the nature of the role?
- Are there strong non-financial incentives to work at your company?
- Do you ask yourself why someone wants to work for you?
  - If the only answer is 'for the money' then your business has problems that go beyond your remuneration structure

The KPI Creation Process

Defining effective sales KPIs can feel like an intimidating process because you're stating how you want your salespeople to focus their time. KPIs need to be tailored to your team, your processes and the objectives you want to achieve, which means creating them from scratch. It can be helpful to check out the KPIs used by other organisations similar to your own, but if you use them as a base, you must make sure yours are specific to your needs.

1. Understand what makes an effective KPI

A key performance indicator is a measurement of success against your business objectives. But what does that really mean and do your sales people know exactly what it means?

The key word here is 'indicator'. Your KPIs should be an indication for what the future holds.

Current metrics measure what is happening right now, historical metrics show what has already happened. Although the KPIs should be focused on current metrics, you need as much historical information as you can get. This will give you the data you need to develop your activity levels, which in turn, will influence your future.

Current Metrics
Discovery Calls
Lead Conversions
Director Level Meetings

Historical Metrics
Average Deal Size
Close Rate
Share of Wallet

Current metrics are controllable behaviour for your sales team's actions. They can be monitored in real time and adjusted accordingly if the team starts to underperform. Historical metrics, such as average deal size, offer insight and are very important to monitor, but they won't affect your sales team's day-to-day activities and the decisions they make on how to spend their time.

2. Map Out Your Sales Process

Once you and your team understand what effective KPIs are, you can start to define your own. The team's KPIs will depend entirely on the actions and activities that comprise your sales process.

It is helpful to analyse and discover what activities are truly meaningful to the sales process. Pick out a few actions your sales people perform that move a prospect through the pipeline. You might include:

- Face-to-face meetings
- Qualifying leads
- Lead Conversions

These would all work well as defined KPIs to drive focussed behaviour.

Examples of different KPIs for a variety of sales roles:

Telemarketing	Internal Sales	Sales Executive
Prospecting email responses	Prospect Conversations	Calls/Dials
Talk time or conversations	Discovery Calls	Prospect Conversions
Qualified Sales Opportunities created	Proposals sent	Opportunities progression in funnel
Lead conversions	Closed Deals	Closed Deals

The goal of this exercise is to be able to map your organisation's sales process, so you'll end up with a clear view of the behaviour and activities you want to reward.

Example:

Prospect Conversation - Discovery Call - Proposal Sent - Closed Deal

These actions move prospects through your sales process; this is the behaviour you want to encourage to achieve your sales objectives so these would work well as KPIs.

3. Reverse Engineer Your Sales Forecast

Now that you've established your KPI activities it is time to look through your historical data to determine how much of each activity it takes to get to the next step of each process. In simple terms, calculate the average number of proposals you submit to achieve one closed deal.

Example:

On average, based on two years of data, submission of four proposals results in one closed deal. Conversion rate = 25%.

Using the same historical data, analyse your sales goal for the month, quarter or year. Using that number work backwards through your sales process to define how many of each activity you need to reach your goal. In the example used above this would be prospect conversation, discovery call, proposal sent, closed deal.

If your sales goal is £1million and your historical metric that tells you your average deal size is £100,000. You will need ten deals to reach your sales goal.

10 deals at the average for your company of £100,000 per deal = £1million

This example shows you how to create a workable, achievable KPI for your sales team. In this example, the sales team must close ten deals to bring in £1million. This becomes the team KPI.

4. Calculate Activities Needed To Achieve the Revenue Target

Calculate the number of activities needed for each step of the process leading up to the final goal. Divide the goal metric by the conversion rate to determine how much of the preceding activity is required.

Using the previous example, start with ten demonstrations. In this example we calculated a 25% conversion rate, divide the ten demonstrations by 0.25 to establish that 40 discovery calls would need to be made.

10 deals 0.25(conversion rate) = 40 discovery calls

You might assume a 25% conversion rate for each part of the process, which would result in:

640 Leads - 160 Conversations - 40 Discoveries - 10 Deals - £1Million

It is now easy to see the quantity of each individual activity required to reach your sales goal. These metrics are your sales KPIs.

It is vital to involve your salespeople early in the process to create visibility around the KPIs. As you track towards your goal be prepared to revise, rewrite and reboot the KPIs when needed to keep your sales people motivated and engaged.

Sales KPI Descriptions

Monthly sales growth	Cost per lead by each channel
Monthly sales/new customers	Cost of a new client by each channel
Monthly new leads/prospects	Hourly/daily/weekly/monthly/quarterly/annual sales
Number of qualified leads	Average conversion time
Resources spent on one non-paying client	Lead-to-close rate: all channels
Resources spent on one paying client	Customer turnover rate
Customer lifetime value	Number of monthly sales demonstrations
Customer profitability	Customer engagement level
Lead-to-sale conversion rate	Number of abandoned shopping carts
Shopping cart abandonment rate	Number of monthly quotes/orders
Average purchase value	Sales by lead source
Average order value	Inbound calls handled per representative
Sales per representative	Outbound calls handled per representative
Average annual sales volume per customer	Average monthly sales volume per customer
Relative market share	Product/service usage every day
Value of returned goods and warranties	Asset turnover ratio (sales to assets)
Percentage of total sales from existing customers	Sales reps per £100k revenue
Monthly sales quota attainment	Sales quota attainment by sales representative
Number of client accounts per account manager	Days sales outstanding

Sales Culture and Collaboration

I like to consider myself as the eternal optimist, but it's true that if you have a bad apple in your barrel, it won't be long before they're all rotten. Nothing spreads through a company quicker than the poison from a negative person with a bad attitude.

As a colleague once said to me 'I would rather have a hole in the business than an arsehole in the business'. I've had a couple of unsavoury experiences with staff that I could and should have acted on earlier if I'd known then what I know now. I have realised that good people want to work with other good people. Clever people are a great asset to your business but only if they are prepared to share their knowledge. Being collaborative creates a culture that is caring and supportive and is set up for success.

Goal: *To ensure there is a positive culture and a commitment to best practice in the sales team.*

Discovery: *Do you encourage and reward behaviour that supports a positive attitude in your sales team to help achieve your goals?*

Your employees have a core of knowledge and experience vital to your success, but equally important, is how much they embrace your company culture and set of values. These underpin how they perform, and their ability to contribute to the business achieving its goals. Your employees need to be positive and engaged and your company culture is responsible for this.

Elements that contribute to your sales culture:

Ability – Do your salespeople have the technical knowledge to perform their role effectively - have you hired the right people and is your training and development programme adequate?

Knowledge – Do they know what is expected of them - is your communication effective?

Motivation – Do your salespeople know why they are doing what they do and understand where it fits into the overall plan for your business - do they know your company's vision and sales targets?

Management – Is the behaviour of the salespeople monitored to ensure that they are demonstrating the attitude that will contribute to the success of the business - do they have regular meetings and 1 on 1s with their manager?

Attitude is the key to creating the right culture. Your employees need to be engaged and positive to demonstrate the behaviour you want, if they are disengaged they might go through the motions or simply tick the boxes for their managers. This will contribute to a poor sales culture, which will work against you achieving your sales goals.

While there is an art to selling and it's true that certain personality types are more suited to the role, there are also processes and techniques in which even 'natural' salespeople need to be trained. Employees that resist or grudgingly accept the need for training might tick the 'attended that course' box for HR, but will not implement the skills learned. Their attitude will sap the energy and enthusiasm of the rest of the sales team and start to spread.

Fostering a culture that is consistent with the aims of the business and creating an environment where knowledge and best practice are shared is vital. Individual salespeople bring different attributes, experiences, skills and approaches to a team. Your best sales people need to be encouraged to share their insights with all team members in a supportive, collaborative environment, otherwise your business will not benefit. This could be something as broad as the way they approach a particular part of the sales process, or as specific as the way they handle particular client objections. Partnering your sales stars with new salespeople, allowing your less experienced staff a front row seat to watch an expert colleague in action, is an excellent way to share tactics and strategies that are proven to work and will encourage good working relationships in the team. If you fail to support a collaborative culture in your sales team, a feeling of elitism may start to develop, allowing experienced and successful salespeople to stand apart from the rest. When they exit your business, they take their knowledge with them and it is lost to you for good.

ACTIONS:

- Regularly analyse whether your salespeople are demonstrating desirable attitudes and are equipped with the necessary skills to sell your products and achieve your company's goals

- Spend time with them in field and see how they perform in front of customers. This also gives you an opportunity to speak to them and understand them as individuals

- Undertake regular skills audits and knowledge management reviews for each team member. These will reveal areas of strength and weakness. The reviews should cover:

  - Product knowledge
  - Sales skills
  - Attitude
  - Motivation
  - Overall work
  - Personal strengths

- Incorporate them into a regular review process on overall performance that goes beyond simply asking whether a salesperson has hit their numbers. You can reinforce what is discovered through training and practice. It is vital for employees to understand why they are having regular reviews and to see them as a measurement of their performance in addition to part of a longer-term development plan. Forcing training on your salespeople without a clear rationale will be ineffective.

- Desirable behaviour should be rewarded appropriately. If your star salesperson makes it part of their job to share best practice and mentor others, you must recognise and reward them. This behaviour is a gift to creating an inclusive culture.

Your company's culture, values and brand, set the tone and create an environment in which people want to work. Regular staff reviews and meetings, where the motivation of employees can be explored, are a good way to discover whether non-financial incentives are present within your company.

Process

Operational structure is needed to ensure growth is sustainable and sales success is repeatable. While vision and the right people for the job are two key ingredients in business success, you also need a clear and consistent process to ensure your products and services are reaching the people who need them. You also have to make sure you can do it again, and again, and again, each time with the same high quality results.

Being familiar with the market in which they operate, and knowing who their customers are, will allow the sales staff to understand what their customers need. Sales and marketing alignment is particularly important with increasing interaction between companies and their customers via social media. Marketing campaigns have changed enormously, with online platforms creating a whole new space in which customers can be reached directly by effective marketing campaigns. It is not unusual for a well-informed customer to be quite far along their buying journey before they even speak to a sales person. If sales and marketing are presenting the same message with the same goal, this can be a good thing. It can enable a quick sale and satisfied customer, but if they are out of alignment, it can result in miscommunication, unreasonable expectations, dropped leads, unqualified leads being pursued too far or customers simply unsatisfied when their expectations exceed what's actually possible.

A consistent process, or methodology, will improve your customer experience and match expectation with result. When your sales staff are secure in their sales structure and process they will sell with less effort and more confidence. Knowing what works and what doesn't will save time and money because dropping leads will become an unusual occurrence, not an accepted cost of doing business.

Process is the engine room of your sales function. It ensures your sales staff are using learnable, repeatable, measurable and consistent methods, specifically designed to achieve your company's objectives.

Vision	People	Process	Management
Alignment to Corporate Strategy	Roles and Responsibility	**Sales and Marketing Alignment**	Forecasting Metrics and KPIs
Value Proposition	Hiring and Onboarding	**Methodology and Winning Customers**	Sales Meetings and Structures
Addressable Market	Training and Development	**Maximising Lifetime Value**	Performance Management
Competitive Landscape	Salary Commission and Bonuses	**CRM and Technology**	Strategic Sales Planning
Go To Market Strategy	Culture and Knowledge Sharing	**Documentation and Collateral**	Integration with the Wider Business

The five key elements are:

Sales and Marketing Alignment
- Do you have an effective and documented way of aligning your sales and marketing initiatives?

Methodology and Winning Customers
- Is there a sales methodology – documented or otherwise that sales staff follow?

Maximising Lifetime Customer Value
- Does your sales process maximise your customer lifetime value?

Customer Relation Management and Technology
- Is there an effective process for customer relation management and are sales people trained to use it and other technological tools?

Documentation and Collateral
- How current is your collateral, how do you update it and is your website responsive and customer friendly?

Sales and Marketing Alignment

I've been invited to many events where the dress code required is smart casual or business casual. I've always had a problem with those descriptions because I think the actual words are contradictory. In my view, smart and business are entirely different from casual. I used it once in a sales talk as an example of lack of alignment between sales and marketing. To illustrate, I keyed the expression 'smart casual' into Google images and was amazed at the variation of interpretations ranging from scruffy tee shirts and shorts to three piece suits.

Goal: *To investigate whether you have a clear policy for lead generation.*

Discovery: *Do you know what kind of leads and customers you want, do you know where your leads come from and are they delivering the kinds of customers you want?*

To start to unravel the complexity that is lead generation it is helpful to ask yourself:

- What is a lead? The inability to define a lead can be major stumbling block for your business. Are you including names that appear on your database because they're in the right industry or because they were customers years ago? These might be leads but not all will be convertible. If you have too many of the wrong type of leads you will waste time, create unrealistic expectations and perhaps miss out on more productive leads.

- What do your leads look like? True leads are specific to your company so it's critical to understand what yours look like. The process of qualifying your sales opportunities starts here.

- Channels: Where do leads come from? This depends on your sales model and your Go To Market strategy. How do you start conversations with potential customers? If your GTM strategy is to market direct, you will be generating leads from email, mail shots and cold calling. If your strategy is indirect, you will have a process for working with your channel and distribution partners. Each model determines the source of leads.

Your business needs a clear process that is cost effective, time efficient, planned and targeted to generate the leads you need.

ACTIONS:

Step 1: Identify the prime source of leads

- Create a matrix of all the ways you acquire leads and see how many are currently used
- Analyse your database of paying customers and identify how the original lead was generated
- If you have no formal lead generation model, work out where the majority of your existing customers came from to provide a default model
- Does this match your Go To Market strategy/plan? If they are not aligned, a rethink is required

- Lead generation needs to be cost-effective. Analyse which routes have generated your most profitable customers. If your most profitable business comes from referrals, could you increase efforts in that area?

Step 2: Qualification

Converting a lead into a real customer takes time, effort and costs money. If you choose to do the hard work of qualifying leads at the beginning of the process you will ensure your resources are put to the best use. What matters is that your leads are put through some kind of filter, whichever lead qualification process you choose. A simple way to qualify a lead is to ask:

- Are they your target customer - your correct buyer persona?
- Are they in the right geographic location – if this is an issue?
- Are they in the correct market segment?
- Are they the right size?
- Have you established whether they have the budget and need for your product/service?
- Do they have the authority to buy?
- Can you accommodate their timescale?

Step 3: Measuring your real pipeline

To make sure your process works properly you should assess the quality of the leads on your database to make sure they are viable and have a customer relation management (CRM) system. Think about:

- How long has the lead been on the database/in your pipeline?
- Has the lead ever made a purchase?
- Has any kind of contact been made with the lead?
- Has the lead ever responded positively by phone, email, through a website download of a case study or white paper?
- If they have been contact, when was the last time?
- Does the lead fit your target customer profile?

Even if a customer is in the right industry, your salespeople should still ask whether your company's offering meets their specific, identifiable need. The goal is to strip out of the pipeline any lead with no realistic prospect of conversion. If you calculate the average conversion time from lead to customer, you will be able to remove leads that are far outside that time and are unlikely to be converted.

Marketing

Marketing should be a key lead driver but Sales Directors don't always systematically review it as often as they should. Your sales and marketing plans need to be aligned to maximise lead generation of your target customers. To find out if you need to make adjustments, consider the following:

- Does your marketing work for you?
- Is it appropriate for your key channels?
- Does it deliver informed and qualified prospects?

- Does it convey a clear value proposition, attracting qualified buyers and discouraging those who will realistically never turn into customers?

Identifying Prospects from Suspects

A good prospect is someone who has a problem that your product can solve efficiently and cost-effectively.
Think about what problems your product or service solves and decide which is the most pressing and valuable. Once you have a clear answer, you will be able to search your marketplace for customers who are likely to have this exact problem.

A good prospect has a goal your product can help them to achieve.
The primary buying motivation for all products and services is improvement. When someone has a desire to improve a specific aspect of his or her life or work and your product or service can help, that someone becomes a very good prospect.

A good prospect has the power to make the buying decision.
It doesn't matter if a prospect has a problem your product can fix, a need your product can satisfy or a goal your product can fulfil, if they don't have the authority to make the decision to buy, then the sale is not going to happen.

A good prospect is someone who likes you and your company, as well as your product.

Despite the anonymity of buying on the Internet, people are primarily emotional in their decision making, particularly in the B2B environment. Almost all emotion revolves around how one person feels about the other. When a prospect argues with you, complains about your products and criticises your company, stay focused and overextend yourself to be polite. You may not win their business, but you will always feel happier and more buoyant when you walk away and there's always another time.

A good prospect is often a centre of influence, someone who can open doors for you to other prospects.
Bending over backwards to acquire a marquee client can pay dividends. One very satisfied customer, who is well known and respected in their marketplace, can create opportunities for you to sell more of your products and services at full price.

A good prospect is easy to sell to especially if they are geographically close.
Delivering satisfaction and building a lasting relationship is much easier when your customer is located nearby. Don't forget to look close to home for prospects; they might be on your own doorstep.

So what does a Suspect look like?

A suspect hasn't told you when they're going to make a decision.
They don't mind wasting your time until they admit they won't be making a decision for months. Nothing wastes more time than someone who ends up saying they're not going to make a decision for months.

A suspect doesn't let you know if they have a need you can help them.
They haven't shared that information with you.

A suspect leaves you unsure if they're the decision maker.
They don't confirm that they can make the decision to buy and your ability to close the sale drops dramatically if you're dealing with someone who is only conveying information to the real decision maker

A suspect doesn't share if they have the financial ability to buy.
They seem sincere and obviously they want your product or service but you don't know if they can afford it.

A suspect has been to a competitor who has helped develop their expectations.
You're asked to respond to the RFP/tender/ bid quote. If you didn't help write the RFP/tender/bid, it is highly likely that your competition has already influenced the deal.

Check Sales Reports Against Buyer Personas

You should have already have created your buyer personas – your typical or target customer. If you refine your buyer personas so thoroughly that you can identify their age, hobbies and a job, your lead generation will be more effective. It is ideal to have four or five target buyer personas.

To check that your buyer personas are correct consider:

- Are prospects that convert matching your anticipated buyer personas?
- What are the behavioural qualifications of your conversions?
  - o Did they linger on your sales page longer than average
  - o Did they make contact
  - o Did they download materials

Observe industry changes because your buyer personas may change as the industry changes. Monitor the market and reassess. Revisit your results and update at least every quarter and document your findings.

Understand the needs of your sales team

Now that you have refined your buyer personas you'll be able to determine whether or not a prospect that fits the criteria and should be considered a lead.

Consider:

- How likely is it that anyone who fits this persona would convert?

- What are other qualifiers that would need to exist for you to feel confident you could close the sale?

- How many of the criteria could be missing for the prospect to remain viable?

- How many of the criteria need to be met to make it a viable prospect?

- Can marketing tactics weed out those who fit the buyer persona but are missing other qualifiers?

- How many of the qualifiers do your Sales team want satisfied before they'll tackle a lead?

- Is your Sales department getting enough leads - if they're not, do you think you should relax your qualifications?

- Is your Sales department swamped with leads that don't convert - if they are, do you think you should increase the criteria to be met before sales approach a lead?

Once you have a solid foundation for determining what your Sales team considers a qualified lead, ask your Marketing department how they qualify a lead. Marketing might qualify anyone who has taken any action, but this won't necessarily match your sales team's criteria for consideration as a viable lead.

Consider:

- Has the lead filled out a form on your website?
- Every time someone takes an action on your website, it should tell you something about them. Only offer things that help identify and qualify a lead.
- Has the lead subscribed to your blog?
- Do they fit some of your buyer persona criteria? Evaluate how much weight that holds for you

- Do you consider someone a lead because they are in the right demographic?

Make sure your sales and marketing teams understand what constitutes a qualified lead to ensure they are both working toward the same objective.

Methodology and Winning Customers

'It's ok Matt I've got my own style for making sales'. I've been told this a few times and as the scars have healed I've concluded that this is actually sales person code for: 'I'm a bit of a maverick and unless I'm given structure I'm going to be a nightmare to manage'. I'm not saying that I want to turn everyone into a clone, far from it, but if you don't have a process already, I suggest you review the best piece of business you've ever done, retrace the steps you took and document it. Show your sales people how you want things done and make sure they're doing it. If and when they have impressed the hell out of you by following your methodology, then maybe you can start giving them more input.

GOAL: *To investigate your approach to lead conversion.*

DISCOVERY: *Do you have a consistent, organised, documented, repeatable process for transforming a lead into a customer?*

Sales is about systems and processes, it is not a mysterious ability possessed by a chosen few. Repeatable processes give all salespeople the best chance of success and are the only foundation on which large businesses can be built. The process is:

- What is actually done to convert a lead into a customer
- Who does it
- The knowledge needed to do it
- The tools required to help achieve the objective

Think about how well your company manages these requirements:

Process
- Do you have a template showing the steps in your sales process from the initial lead to qualification calls, meetings, presentations, negotiation and the close including who is responsible for each part?
- Do all your salespeople convey the same message about your company, your products, your customer offer and your USPs?

Knowledge
- Is the knowledge and experience in your sales team shared consistently and widely?
- Is sales best practice understood, encouraged and embraced?
- Is intelligence about your company's customers captured and made available to all who need it?

Tools
- Do you have standardised sales and marketing materials to ensure quality control and maximise efficiency?
- Do your salespeople understand the competitive landscape in which they operate?
- Do they have access to information on key rivals?

ACTION:

Standardise and document your sales approach.

Designing your Sales Process

If you have the right sales process you will be able to capitalise on potential opportunities. Your sales process must be aligned to your products and services, properly documented, communicated to your sales staff and fully understood. Creating your sales process is a key strategy to save your company money, time and resources by ensuring your sales team act in consistently and efficiently. Your process must be trainable, learnable, actionable, consistent and repeatable.

The benefits of having a defined sales process include:

- Increased customer satisfaction
- Increased referral capability
- Lower staff turnover because your staff will be more closely aligned to your business aspirations
- Create scale/leverage for your business to grow
- Staff empowerment because your efficient process will reduce the need for micromanagement
- Increased productivity while retaining quality standards

Consider:

- You are the customer, how would you like to be treated?
- Should you have a different process for pre and post Sale, New Business v Account Management?
- Where are the opportunities to excel and allow you to stand out from your competition?

- Does your sales process compliment your USPs and reinforce why your customer buys from you?
- How many steps you need to win a client, don't add more just for the sake of it. All elements of the sales process should progress not prolong the sale.
- The type of touch points you want to use when working with customers and prospects. Identify which method you prefer, one-way: email or two-way: phone and face to face.

Tips to help you design and implement your Sales Process

- Make sure all processes and outcomes are written down or drawn in a flow chart

- If you're a visual learner, using Post It notes when designing your process will allow you to switch and change the order of steps

- Make sure all steps are mirrored

- Get your team members involved in designing the process. It's important to understand what really happens in your business and not rely solely on reporting or management commentary

- Review your data usage and assess any improvements you could make to your IT systems

- Consider if automating simple, repetitive tasks by using technology will improve your process

- When it's ready, communicate the sales process to all staff, not just those involved in sales

Things to consider when your process is in place

- If you're losing business, analyse at what stage in your process it occurs. Tighten up any weaknesses you find to cut down on sales leakage

- Consider your negotiation steps and identify any products and services in your offering which, despite having a high perceived value, cost you very little – this will protect your margin and profit

- Schedule a regular review of your sales process for continuous improvement

- Look for opportunities to get a referral to a new customer

- Remember that it's easier to sell to an existing customer than a new one

The Value of Effective Sales Qualification

Effective qualification can dramatically improve your sales. Let's take an in-depth look at sales qualification because it is vital to your growth and profit to understand it fully.

Qualification is of paramount importance in the sales process because poor qualification costs the business more than any other single part of the sales process. You will spend time, effort and in some cases company money, tempting a window shopper if you fail to determine that the prospect is a serious potential buyer. The unqualified prospect is potentially someone just enjoying the free lunch and an invitation to the football, or they might even work for your closest competition, conducting competitive research.

Identifying that a prospective customer wants to buy your product is the first step in an effective sales process. A qualified prospective customer will have the means, motive and desire to buy. If they qualify on these three points then you are justified in spending your company's time and resources to work to close the sale.

What should I look for when I am qualifying a customer?

When you qualify a customer you must ensure that you have enough information to make an informed decision. An opportunity would include:

- Interest from the prospect to the sale
- Identification of the decision maker or makers in the company and confirmation that they are interested
- Initial research to match the customer to the product or service and ensure that it is of value to them

There are many systems used to qualify leads: BANT, SCOTSMAN and CHAMP are the most well known and they all have strengths and weaknesses depending on various factors including industry, product and service. Whether a unique methodology is developed or an industry recognised one is used, it is vital that all your sales team use the same method of qualification to enable like for like measurement.

What is the difference between BANT, SCOTSMAN and CHAMP?

The difference between the three systems is how they are applied. They will all identify what is needed to determine the strength and viability of an opportunity but have different priorities.

BANT – Budget, Authority, Need, Timeline was developed by IBM in the 1960s and revolutionised the sales process when it was introduced. The balance of power changed and customers had to prove they were viable opportunities, or sales staff would not waste their time with them. In today's more sophisticated market BANT is considered too simple, unable to address complex company buying processes that may have multiple decision makers.

CHAMP - Challenges, Authority, Money, Prioritisation. A company called Insightsquared introduced this system in 2014. CHAMP addresses qualification by emphasising the customer's challenge, what pain and need are leading them to consider buying. It operates in the opposite way to BANT focusing on the need to buy, not the ability to pay for the product or service.

SCOTSMAN - Solution, Competition, Originality, Timescale, Size, Money, Authority, Need.
This methodology of qualification has evolved to match business trends. SCOTSMAN qualification requires a deeper look into more aspects of a potential customer and gives a more informed evaluation of their buying

readiness and appetite. The acronym can be read as follows:

Solution: What is the value of the product or service relative to the client's need? Does it provide them with a solution?

Competition: Who are we competing with for the sale? Has the client expressed an interest in a competitor's offering and where do we stand in relation to the main competition?

Originality: What unique benefits does the product or service provide? Have they been communicated to the client?

Timescale: Does the client's timescale match what is possible to provide? Do they work with our needs?

Size: What is the scope of the opportunity and is there enough potential? Does it fit with our sales targets?

Money: Does the client have budget to buy the product or service?

Authority: Is the person the decision maker or someone able to authorise the purchase?

Need: Does the client recognise their need for the product or service? Has the need been sufficiently communicated and discussed?

How Do You Choose The Best Methodology?

The best salespeople ask the right questions, to get the right information, using any of the qualifying methodologies as a guide not a checklist.

An effective salesperson will discover all the important qualifying criteria through natural conversation. They will ask questions, analyse the answers and then ask more questions. Through the course of organic conversation, the salesperson will discover whether a given lead is a potential client. In addition to this, the salesperson will conduct some of their own research to establish the veracity of the prospect's responses.

Salespeople should be optimists with a healthy dose of scepticism and should not be afraid to challenge a prospect by asking questions that will reveal more depth of information. It is natural to want every lead to turn into a client, but it is more important at the qualifying stage, to have the courage to weed out any prospect that doesn't match the company's qualifying criteria.

What is the right Methodology?

There is no right methodology there is only a right way of using the methodology you choose. Leaders must develop a qualifying methodology to determine a lead's purchasing capacity, needs and process. The best, brightest and most creative sales people will lean on their own experience and strengths to qualify prospects.

Consistency is more important than which methodology you choose

It doesn't matter which methodology is used to gather qualifying criteria, but it does matter that every team member implements the method consistently, every time. This consistency is crucial for these reasons:

- To create a uniform measurement to assess the progress of the sales team

- To maintain continuity in the customer experience

- To provide a consistent qualifying template for scaling

- To present a consistent method of qualification as part of the onboarding and training for new sales staff

Consistent sales success depends on sizing up opportunities and focussing on the ones with the greatest potential. Doing anything else is a waste of valuable time, energy and company resources. Once your methodology is in place, don't get hoodwinked into letting your sales people tell you how busy they are and how many deals they're following up – be rigorous and ask questions of them to ensure they are qualifying their opportunities. Asking the right questions may lead to them not being as busy as they think they are!

Process Template Sample

New Customer Enquiry	First Interaction	Next Step	Next Step	Next Step	Next Step	Next Step
How does a new customer initially engage with your company and what do they do at this stage?						
What is the first thing you do to engage with the customer and what is their very first experience?						
Who does this in your business? Are they the best people to do this and are they trained to do so?						
What actions do you take to further qualify the potential sales opportunity in or out?						
What is your preferred method of communication e.g. phone, email, face to face, at this specific stage?						
What does your company do and what do your people do at this stage to stand out from your competition ?						

What about the maverick rock star that insists their way is the only way?

There will always be a maverick following their own way to achieve results and reluctant to change. If this is true of your top sales person, evaluate what they do and how they do it and consider that they might be right not to change. Examine their statistics carefully. Are they achieving consistent results? Are they actually way ahead of the rest of the sales team? If the figures do stack up and you believe it is their method that is producing their outstanding performance then it would be wise to switch your whole team to it. Document and provide training to all sales staff because whatever methodology you choose, it must be teachable, learnable, consistently applied and everyone must use it.

Prospects vs. Suspects: Identify the Leads Worth Pursuing

All leads are prospects until qualification reveals them to be suspects who don't have the budget, authority, need or timeline to make them worth chasing. Thorough qualification will save you time effort and money, a suspect wastes all three whether they mean to or not. In addition, now you're not disappearing up an alley chasing a suspect, you'll be free to follow a qualified prospect to close the sale.

Consistently applied, sales qualification is an efficient way for staff to determine how to prioritise their time. The best, brightest and most creative sellers will lean on their own experience and strengths to qualify prospects in and suspects out. They will identify the opportunities that need more time because they are stronger or more lucrative, and will waste less time pursuing leads that are unlikely to be closed or to contribute to the company's overall strategy.

Improved results from deploying a good qualification system will help to reduce bad habits in sales staff. Effective training and coaching of a qualifying methodology will ensure sales staff will determine whether the prospect is a good fit, and where they are on their buying journey, before approaching them to outline the features and benefits of their product or service. Short cuts to try to close the sale will be unnecessary as sales staff will be confident that the prospect is viable.

Whatever the reason, the cost of failing to qualify prospects and opportunities effectively, comes at an enormous cost to the company and the sales people they employ.

Closing problems or simply poor sales qualification?

When analysing sales performance, it is tempting to look at leaky pipelines and declining conversion rates and determine sales staff have a problem with closing. Closer analysis will often reveal the reason is poor qualification. Tom Hopkins International, evaluated the selling skills of more than two hundred thousand sales people and found that the biggest difference between the top performers and those just getting by, was in their lead qualification.

Effective qualification will fix most closing problems, eliminating the need to apply pressure and hard close prospects that are not a good fit or not ready to buy. It will enable sales staff to recognise where the prospect is in the buying cycle and not pursue them to a close if they're not ready. Instead, only prospects that need, can afford and will benefit from the product or service will be at the closing stage. The close will be natural and easy without the need for gimmicks or high-pressure tactics.

Top performers know and understand the correlation between qualification and closing and continue to refine their qualification skills. Average performers may be unaware of how qualification feeds into the close and have not developed this vital skill in the sales process, or they might simply ignore qualification preferring to rely on gut feeling. A salesperson who relies on their gut feel should be treated with extreme caution.

Every professional salesperson should understand that qualification is a core competency and that the process and methods for qualifying can easily be learnt. Investing in more training and coaching for your sales leaders and staff to develop this essential competency in essential. The cost and impact of failing to do so will show in your sales and profits.

Are your Sales Cycles getting longer and conversion rates declining?

Ask yourself if your company boasts a big pipeline of opportunities that never close or worse still disappear from the radar. As the market continues to evolve, becoming more sophisticated, business owners and sales leaders are acutely aware that selling is becoming more difficult as buyers become more educated. Increasingly often, a buyer's journey is well advanced before they even engage with a sales person. In this evolution customers have embraced a new way of researching and buying but companies' sales processes often remained unchanged.

The Best Salespeople Ask the Right Questions to Get the Right Information

An experienced and effective salesperson who is fully aware of the value of qualification discovers all the important qualifying criteria through natural conversation. They ask questions, analyse the answers, and then ask more questions. During an organic conversation, the salesperson will discover whether their lead qualifies as a genuine prospect.

Ultimately prospects buy things because they have a specific need or challenge. Specific qualification questions and active listening will uncover these needs. Knowing which questions to ask and what specific answers to listen for is the key to successful qualifying and moving a prospect to the next stage of the sales pipeline.

What are the right questions and why are you asking them?

Individual style and experience will dictate how a sales person opens the discussion but generally the logical way to start is with general or big picture questions.

General Questions (Needs/Challenges)

- What is the biggest challenge facing your business?
- How long have you had this challenge?
- What's prompting you to address it now?

- What has prevented you from addressing it before?
- Have you tried to solve it?
- Why didn't the solution work?
- What are the likely consequences if this remains unresolved?
- What are some of the hurdles that may stop you from resolving it?

These questions aim to establish what the major challenge is, the cause of the challenge, the effect if they do nothing and whether they've attempted to resolve it without success. The answers will trigger more questions or reveal if there's no real problem and so no real reason to buy. At any point the sales person can disqualify the lead or in conversation, explain to the customer from an external viewpoint, the danger of not resolving the issue.

Budget questions (Money)

- Has a budget been agreed for this purchase?
- Are we within those budget parameters?
- Are there any competing projects for this budget allocation?
- Are there any close competitors for the sale?

Budget isn't everything but it must be a significant factor in qualification. Although it's not appropriate to negotiate at this stage of the relationship, it is important to understand if the offering and the ability to pay are in the same range.

Authority questions (Decision process)

- Who will be involved in making the decision to purchase?
- How are purchasing decisions made and who will be involved in making the final decision?
- Where does this sit amongst the decision maker's current priorities?
- Do you think the other decision makers will have any concerns?
- What concerns do you think they may have?
- How do you think we should handle their concerns?
- Would it make sense to schedule a meeting to answer any questions they may have?

If and when it is known that there are additional financial decision makers, these people need to be included in the conversations as soon as possible. Make sure it is clear who does what. If there is a committee involved, it is important to know who has the authority to sign off and who gives the spend financial approval.

Timeline questions

- What is your timeline for making this decision?
- Is getting this resolved now a priority for you?
- How quickly do these results need to be achieved?
- What other solutions are you evaluating?

This set of questions will provide information about how urgently a solution is required. It will also reveal if the prospect is considering another offering. Further questions are needed to find out if they are serious about your offering or trying to put pressure on price with the other provider. Active listening and more probing should tell you if their interest is sincere.

Specific questions

- Of all the factors we have discussed, what's most important to you?

- Have I covered every detail that's important to you?

- What are you looking for in a supplier?

- How will you measure success?

- Does solving this problem have an impact on you personally?

- Based on our discussion, does our offering meet your needs?

Customer expectations are critical in every stage of the engagement. Good communication will allow measurement of what expectations are and whether they're being met. To turn a prospect into a happy customer, their expectations must be met or if possible exceeded. Conversely, if their definition of success doesn't match what you know your solution will provide, you must consider disqualifying the prospect.

If your first conversation shows a personal interest by the customer, they will be more effective when they argue for your offering if approval is by a financial committee. The more impact for them in not finding a solution, the more likely they are to become your champion.

The Importance of Continuous Qualification

Smart sales staff will revisit the sales qualification process on a regular basis with the opportunities they're pursuing. It is important to keep abreast of any changes that can make a big difference to the viability of a qualified lead. Sales teams need to build a good relationship with their prospects so they can adjust their efforts accordingly and will know immediately if a red flag pops up.

My Lead Has Become Unqualified – Now What?

This isn't always a disaster and if qualification has been monitored, it won't be a total surprise. Revisiting the sales qualification process will generate new questions and new information that may accelerate a sales opportunity or reinvigorate a stalled situation.

The update can help to reallocate time and focus for maximum return. A lead that has switched to unqualified for budgetary or other reasons can be moved to a different contact priority. It is good practice to revisit the customer or keep in contact via email. Unqualified opportunities can revert to fruitful opportunities in the future as a result of re-qualifying.

Effective Sales Qualification and the Right Frame of Mind

The last piece of the puzzle in the qualification process is the right frame of mind. The picture is nearly complete with the sales people trained, a consistent process properly embedded and targets looking achievable. The right frame of mind, in addition to an effective and consistent qualification process, are key elements in a successful sales environment.

Changing the focus from winning a sale to helping a customer to take advantage of the collaborative nature of the qualification conversation will make strategic and tactical plans more effective.

Qualification must not be seen as a trick to close a sale, but the opening of a collaborative relationship with a customer, which may provide them with new ideas or a different perspective. When a properly qualified prospect is engaged in this way the sale should be closed in a natural and easy manner.

Remembering that poor qualification costs the business more than any other single part of the sales process, allows your sales team to focus on viable sales, consistently meet their targets and build the company's growth and profit.

Maximising Customer Lifetime Value

I spent months developing a relationship with the finance director of a company and eventually won them as a client. The project and system was going really well and the finance director loved the product and what we were doing. I visited a couple of times for review meetings and we discussed future phases over a working lunch. I didn't realise it at the time, but I wasn't engaging with enough other people in the company. It all started to fall apart when a new Commercial Director with a wider remit to review systems was appointed. I couldn't get in to meet him and after numerous phone calls, I found out that the finance director been forced out as part of a power struggle – but worse was yet to come, we were given notice that our system was going to be replaced in its entirety, as part of a new corporate technology project.

GOAL: *To investigate how effectively your company follows through with customers post-sale to exploit fully the lifetime revenue opportunity of the relationship.*

DISCOVERY: *Are your sales people given the responsibility and the tools for managing a lifetime relationship with your customers?*

It is usually easier to sell to existing customers than new ones, so it makes sense to extend the lifetime value of your customers. Accounts need to be developed to maximise opportunities through repeat business including cross selling and up selling. There are several considerations that will help or hinder you:

Balance

Your revenue might be split between one-off sales that require a constant search for new clients and repeat business selling to your existing customers. Ideally, you should seek a balance between the two. If you just chase new customers, disregarding the potential for repeat sales, you are losing an opportunity to maximise the value of your customers and stabilise a stream of revenue. If you fail to prospect for new customers your business will be at risk. Neither extreme is healthy.

What do you sell?

Whether you are able to create lifetime relationships will depend on your industry. Whether it is usual for your business only to make one-off sales, such as double-glazing, or at the other extreme, a consultancy that works with clients over the long term and rarely needs to prospect, then your sales strategy should reflect that. Most businesses however will not be at either extreme and your sales strategy should be appropriate for your situation.

Sales structure

Some businesses miss out on repeat business, not because the product precludes it, but because they aren't set up to exploit lifetime value.

ACTION:

- Establish what your customer revenue model looks like

Calculate your revenue split between new and repeat customers, then consider what the mix should be. Given the nature of your product, do you think more revenue should be coming from repeat customers? Are there additional purchases that should flow on naturally after the first sale and does that happen after a given period? Are there cross-selling and up-selling opportunities with the same customer and are they being optimised?

- Key Account Plans

A Key Account Management Plan will provide you with a structure for securing the maximum lifetime value from a customer. The plan incorporates everything you know about your customer and your relationship with them. It will include an overall SWOT analysis of your company in relation to that customer, the commercial history of the account and an outline of the strategic and tactical approach with overall objectives. When you recognise a repeat business opportunity you must have an effective sales strategy.

- People

The Key Account Plan will only be successful if you have the right sales person to implement a lifetime value approach. To optimise the knowledge and personal connection that drives repeat sales, you should consider the type of individual best suited to managing the customer in the long term. This might not be the salesperson that made the original sale. Winning sales and developing long-term business are two different skill-sets. The personality suited to hunting down and converting new leads is generally not the one to nurture a long-term relationship. Think about changing your Key

Account managers periodically. It's possible for the manager to become too familiar with the customer and in concentrating on the relationship they forget to ask the big question – 'How can I help you meet your goals?'. A fresh pair of eyes is likely to see opportunities that would otherwise be missed and breathe new life into the customer relationship.

- Rewards

The lifetime customer value concept will affect your remuneration policy. Salespeople need different incentives for different roles. The incentive and KPIs required to motivate and reward a sales person whose primary role is to win new business, will be very different from those that will reward and motivate a person to generate repeat sales. You might also factor in cross selling opportunities, where a sales person will highlight an opportunity to sell to another salesperson's customer. To encourage that kind of behaviour, salespeople should be rewarded for earning additional revenue for your business.

- Systems – technology

To facilitate long-term account management you will need to invest in a good Customer Relationship Management system. If you want to develop long-term strategic partnerships you will need to understand who does what in your customer's organisation and be able to meet their specific needs. It is essential that all customer contact and intelligence is captured and recorded to maximise cross-selling and up-selling opportunities or at least, to ensure that opportunities are not lost. A good Customer Relationship Management system will help to build a full picture of each customer, their organisation and the history of your relationship with them.

- Systems - organisation

To be successful with long-term customer value you will need an appropriate internal organisational structure. Sales meetings need to be set up to consider repeat selling opportunities as well as new lead conversion.

CRM and Technology

'Hello, is that Mr Garman?' – wow, I thought when the man answered the phone at the garden centre. I'd only rung them once before and I needed some more materials to finish my garden renovations. 'How did you know it was me?' 'We took down your number when you placed your last order and our system pops up the details if it recognises the number.' I was impressed, I felt valued and made the decision then and there to continue to use them.

GOAL: *To investigate whether your company's technology supports your sales process.*

DISCOVERY: *Does your company have the tools to drive the key elements of sales?*

All companies need technology to support all three parts of the selling process. The tools run in tandem with the sales process to reinforce the understanding that it's a structured, repeatable, teachable skill not game of chance or luck.

The main features of a sales organisation and the tools that support it:

Getting leads

The way we do business is evolving all the time and Sales and Marketing processes and tools have had to change to ensure they are able to be effective in a new market place. Potential customers may be a considerable way into their buying journey before your company has the opportunity to be in contact with them.

They need to be engaged at the top of the funnel and then again in the middle, to make this happen, we need to rely on technological tools.

Converting leads into customers

Leads are expensive to create. The journey to conversion is a complex, multi-faceted process. Technology is a vital part of ensuring you can get the maximum value out of every lead. After a lead has been captured, the ability to convert will be largely dependent on your CRM system and email marketing. If you don't segment properly and use rule-based follow-up with leads, they will be difficult to qualify and convert. Email marketing is driven by the analysis of customer interaction with your website.

Maximising lifetime value

It costs more to acquire a new customer than to sell to an existing one and the tools that assist with repeat sales are invaluable. They can nurture and monitor engagement with your business, analysing a customer's browsing history on your website to deliver highly targeted content to provide cross-selling and up-selling opportunities.

There are two types of tools: those that assist with some aspect of the sales process and those that are repositories for information about your customers and your company's interaction with them. Your choice of sales tools will depend on the nature of your business, but irrespective of industry, every organisation needs a CRM to underpin their sales process, allowing data to be held, organised and updated in a central repository.

The consequences of not having an adequate CRM will hamper your ability to grow your sales, profit and reputation. Disadvantages to working without a CRM system include:

- Opportunities missed and time and resources wasted
- Data held in spread sheets will have to be copied across to other sheets and updated manually, increasing the risk of human error
- Data held by individual salespeople won't be shared
- Information managed by individuals will exit your company when that person goes
- Lost opportunities for up and cross selling
- No database of customers owned, controlled and managed by your business

ACTION:

- A CRM system is the key tool. If you want to grow your business, improve your sales and profit you must choose a system and start rolling it out as soon as possible

- There are many other technical tools available to assist at all stages of your sales process.

  - Specialist lead generation tools enable direct communication with leads who visit your website, displaying customised messages when certain conditions are met

- Tools that boost the percentage of visitors completing web forms

- Tools that use the IP address to identify companies viewing your website even if they don't fill out an enquiry form

- Lead conversion tools allow you to track every interaction a lead has with your website and then use them as triggers for an email marketing campaign

- Your company may already have some of these tools so you should audit what you have to establish which are being used and how extensively and effectively. Tools are often under-utilised, wasting money and opportunities. It is usually because they are either the wrong tool or the sales force have not been trained to use them and are unaware of their benefits

- If you can't make a clear business case to buy a tool, don't buy it; it's likely to be the wrong one if you cannot identify a specific and relevant benefit. Tools will only add value if they make your sales peoples' lives easier. Ensure you have a procedure for analysing the cost and benefits of investment that involves consultation with your sales staff. If they don't or won't use them, you will be wasting your money

- To ensure tools are fully utilised, training and demonstrations of the benefits must be given to all sales staff. If your staff can see the benefit of the tool they will use it

- A large part of customer relationship management is determining a metric for success. Forecasting lets you know a benchmark by which you can determine whether your results are actually on par with your efforts.

Documentation and Collateral

I once went to a business that designed and installed new canopies for petrol stations. They were planning an upgrade to their IT system and I was hoping to secure them as a client. I was intrigued by their business and started asking how they won their customers.
'Well, it's quite tough sometimes, we have to do lots of technical specifications, designs and drawings - even at the early stage'.
I introduced them to a digital camera, Photoshop and a dye sublimation printer. We transformed their dull, lengthy description text only proposals to much leaner and more powerful proposals that actually showed a prospect 'what it looks like today' and 'what it will look like when we're finished'. It was one of my best ever sales.

GOAL: *To review and audit the tools, materials and collateral you use in your sales and marketing process.*

DISCOVERY: *What key pieces of documentation do you use in your sales process?*

It is essential to use standardised documentation and collateral to support your sales process. Consider the following:

- You must ensure that the correct messages are going out to customers
- Standardised documentation and collateral underpin a consistent sales process ensuring best practices are followed
- Standardisation ensures that your sales people have the most up-to-date materials

- It guarantees employee onboarding and on-going training is consistent
- It maximises the efficiency of the sales team
- All necessary materials should be available online to your sales team
- They must be easy to customise - they won't have to create their own
- It allows for individual character and style but prevents individuals going rogue

The standard materials sales people use in the field must match your company's presence in the public domain.

- Your website should provide supporting sales and marketing materials with content and look consistent with your other collateral
- Your presence on social media - Twitter, LinkedIn, Face book – should project the same consistent message

Materials should cover all parts of the sales funnel:

Awareness – Educational, helpful, informative content to establish your company's credentials as experts in your field

Evaluation – Materials providing more specific information on your product

Purchase – Product demonstration, specific financial information relating to ROI, guides to quotations and estimates

Your materials should be:

Practical: Tools and templates should be intuitive and practical or they will not be used

Accessible: Materials should be stored in a central online location where all sales personnel can access them

Visible: The induction process for new starters in the sales team must include how to use the templates and sales tools with emphasis on their benefits to encourage usage

ACTIONS:

Conduct an overall sales and marketing audit to see what materials are being used in the field. Survey your salespeople to find out what they rely on and ask them if there is anything they don't have that they would find useful.

The audit should cover:

- Templates for use in customer meetings:

  - Presentation
  - Quotation
  - Proposal

- Marketing collateral:

  - Fact and data sheets,
  - Case studies
  - White papers

- Sales aids
- ROI calculators
- Webinars
- Demonstration videos

- Competitor analysis:

  - Sales battlecards on all major competitors

- Web and other electronic collateral

The benchmark for your material is that it must be relevant, current and easy to customise. The material must be useful to your customers and sales staff. Check that it is consistent with your company's value proposition and sales channels. For example, if your company sells a high value product/service or one that requires a high degree of human Interaction, material content designed to sell your product over the Internet will not be appropriate.

Get your sales people to update their sales battlecards regularly and provide feedback on the materials they use so that you know they are still relevant. This should be an integral part of your sales meetings.

Management

If you have strong vision, the right people, and a clear and effective sales process you must have effective management – the ability to monitor and continually improve operations.

Consistent monitoring, including sales metrics and sales based KPIs in the form of comprehensive performance and development reviews, will allow you to pick up any loss of motivation or under performance quickly and take appropriate action. Analysis of customer profitability and your product margins on a regular basis will ensure you're aware of any changes in the market affecting your sales and give you time to address them before they are able to prevent you achieving your targets.

The various challenges in your business will demand your time at random. Without the discipline of a robust process, you might sacrifice too much time attending to trivial matters that became more serious due to lack of early attention. You might need to decide between something urgent and something important. Too many calls on your time like this might mean you have to sacrifice something important to fix an urgent short-term issue.

Consistent management process allows you to plan your time and minimise urgent action taken at the expense of important planned activity. The greater control you have over your time, the greater your ability to work on the things that are important to you.

Your company will benefit from consistent management processes and good integration amongst the different departments in your business. A combined effort, with all departments knowing their value and contribution, will result in more sales and happier customers.

Good management is essential for a sustainable, high performing company.

Vision	People	Process	Management
Alignment to Corporate Strategy	Roles and Responsibility	Sales and Marketing Alignment	**Forecasting Metrics and KPIs**
Value Proposition	Hiring and Onboarding	Methodology and Winning Customers	**Sales Meetings and Structures**
Addressable Market	Training and Development	Maximising Lifetime Value	**Performance Management**
Competitive Landscape	Salary Commission and Bonuses	CRM and Technology	**Strategic Sales Planning**
Go To Market Strategy	Culture and Knowledge Sharing	Documentation and Collateral	**Integration with the Wider Business**

Forecasting, Metrics and KPIs

- Document key metrics with recommendations for improving visibility of sales
- Ensure all staff have KPIs aligned with the sales and marketing strategies

Sales Meetings and Structure

- The structure of the sales department
- How are sales meetings run and how effective are they with areas for improvement

Performance Management

- Performance management for both individuals and teams
- Consistent process aligned with company goals

Strategic Sales Planning

- The process for Sales Planning, who is involved and opportunities for improvement
- Sales Planning must be aligned with company goals

Integration with the Wider Business

- Interaction between Sales and other departments within the company
- Opportunities to build cross company relationships

Before we look at the five elements in this section, we're going to look at the Sales Playbook. The Sales Playbook is an important tool that will help you to keep in mind all that you know about how to grow your business and increase your profit.

Sales Playbook

The Sales Playbook is the home for your documented processes. It is based on your company's experience of selling your product to your specific customer base. It should capture best practice through data analysis of your successful customer conversions and identify how your best salespeople operate.

The Playbook should:

- Contain information on your company's identity and beliefs
- Your value proposition
- Your product offering
- Your pricing strategy
- Information on the market in which you operate
- Guide salespeople through all the stages of the process of converting a lead
- Document the sales process and methodology
- Be clear about who is responsible for each stage of the process
- Show how technology is used within the process - effective CRM use is the starting point but there are many other pieces of software available to streamline the lead conversion process
- Best practice – institutionalising what your best salespeople are already doing e.g. objection handling
- Identify the best responses to repeated issues raised by customers, incorporate them into the playbook
- Document key behaviour for all stages of the sales process to enable use of the combined knowledge base in your business

- Include a guide to all key sales and marketing collateral
- Templates for pitches, proposals, ROI calculators and other materials for client interaction

The list is relatively straightforward but there is a large amount of work to be done to create your truly useful sales playbook. It is worth making the effort to deconstruct your sales process. Your playbook must reflect what is really happening day-to-day in your sales team, based on real data and customer information not reports from your sales managers or sales directors.

Conduct a CRM audit to see how your system is being used and how conscientious your salespeople are in recording their customer interactions. This will show you whether there is a structured approach and how methodical they are in following up leads. It will also indicate if a salesperson is habitually giving up too soon in the process.

Your playbook will only be useful if it is practical, using real experience from your company. It should be introduced to employees during their induction process and its content regularly updated and reinforced with all staff to achieve consistent results.

Sample Sales Playbook

Overview:

- Description of your business and history and your reason for being
- Key milestones from early days to current state

Values and beliefs:

- Your company's core values and beliefs with your founding principles
- The language and identity of your business
- What you expect of your business
- What your customers expect from your business
- The standards that you expect from the people who represent your business

Company Information:

- Key facts and headline statistics
- Main contacts in your business and sales
- Where to find your key information and references - website, Intranet, online file storage

Your Market:

- Your target market and sector - the addressable market
- Routes and channels to market - how you operate
- Ideal client profile - if appropriate, mention the types of business you don't want
- Customer success stories and PR

Your Product and Service offering:

- Your Value Proposition
- How you position your company in the market e.g. Premium or Economy
- Why you operate in your space
- Key features and benefits, be clear and limit to three

Brief Overview of the Competitive Landscape:

- Competitors
- Company information
- SWOT analysis

Pricing:

- Your standard pricing structure
- Price flexibility, negotiation and authority
- When to walk away in a competitive situation

Collateral:

- Overview of brochures/case studies/technical fact sheets
- Proven methodologies
- Online sales aids and digital tools and how they can be accessed

Individual and Team Responsibility:

- Minimum standard expectation level of your sales people
- Training/education and Customer Data Protection requirement
- What it means to be part of your sales department
- Holding others to account and maintaining standards

Process:

- Your sales process and methodology - include references links/URLs
- Why you follow the methodology and the importance of it to your business
- Details of training material and back to basics tools and guides
- Use of technology/effective use of CRM/importance of keeping records

Meetings and Communication:

- Describe the frequency and structure of your sales meetings

- Team mechanics - how you work together
- Individual expectations
- Accepted methods of communication and reporting chains of command

Forecasting, Metrics and KPIs

Selling life insurance is hard work and usually commission only. Routes to market as a new recruit were typically door knocking, cold calling by phone and sometimes standing at the exit of a DIY store on a Sunday morning. You need the skin of a rhinoceros and the ability to stomach being told 'no' hundreds of times a day and 'fuck off' very regularly. It was soul destroying, but I needed the money. I knew I would sell policies eventually and that it was all a question of statistics, so I started to count the rejections to work out my pitch to sales ratio. I needed to be told 'no' or 'fuck off' 249 times before I sold something. I knew my average order was a shade under £500 and I needed to make 250 contacts before I could expect a sale. Now I knew what I was aiming for and how to get there, I happily went about my business collecting '£2 fuck offs'.

GOAL: *To investigate whether your company is measuring the success of your sales team effectively.*

DISCOVERY: *Do the elements of forecasting, metrics and KPIs work together effectively?*

To assess your sales team's success or failure, your managers need to know which numbers to look at and measure them consistently. If you can measure, you can manage – and forecast - effectively. A gut feel assessment is never an option.

Forecasting, metrics and KPIs are all interlinked. Your company's vision and long term goals need to be translated into forecasts – both long and short term. Appropriate metrics must be identified to monitor progress towards the achievement of those forecasts and KPIs must be set for the salespeople responsible for bringing in the necessary revenue.

Long-term revenue and profit targets, for example five years, must be supported by a clear vision of your offer, the size of your customer base, the type of customers you're looking for and your competitors. Your five-year forecast must be broken down into smaller goals, for example 5 x 12 months.

Forecasts:

If you are going to achieve your overall sales target you will need a well thought-out plan. It is not good enough to calculate your sales target by adding a percentage to last year's figure. Realistic forecasts need to go all the way down to the level of individual salespeople and be based on what is happening in the field. There must be a link between the targets and the resources required to hit them, which means you must have a clear plan in order to utilise your sales budget properly otherwise it won't work.

Metrics:

You need to know what you should be measuring and how you should be doing it. This requires a structure and agenda to enable you to manage your sales team's performance if you need to.

KPIs:

Appropriate KPIs have to be applied to ensure salespeople are doing what is required to achieve their targets. Near-term targets can be broken down into individual KPIs. Even the simplest exercise - dividing the revenue target by the number of salespeople – is a valuable first step towards setting individual sales targets.

ACTIONS:

- **Forecasting**

Successful forecasting rests on high-level sales qualification. Forecasts are living systems and should evolve accordingly. A forecast made at the beginning of the financial year and not reviewed until the end is worthless. Unreviewed, it will fail to take into account business trends, external events, changes in your competition and disrupters in your industry.

- You should have a structured and consistent method for qualifying your leads and to ensure they fit your buyer persona
- Consider whether they are they actually in a position to buy, BANT is a simple filter
- SCOTSMAN can be used if you want a more detailed filter

This will only work if the names in your pipeline are reviewed frequently to ensure that they are genuine leads rather than just fillers. An honest examination of your pipeline will reveal a lot of names, including many apparent opportunities that have not been properly qualified. This makes it not a true pipeline but simply a list of people you think you can sell to. The real pipeline – consisting of customers with a realistic prospect of buying something within a reasonable timeframe - is probably much smaller. You should eliminate any unrealistic prospects as quickly as possible to avoid wasted effort.

Consider the following:

- Do you have a process for conducting regular reviews and purging leads that have not turned into sales after a set time period?
- Do all your salespeople provide a regular and accurate sales pipeline analysis?

Converting leads can be the critical barrier to achieving your targets, which rests on whether opportunities are being properly qualified at the beginning of the process. If this doesn't happen, applying a ratio of sales to leads is meaningless.

Accurate forecasting requires a regular check on the status of potential deals in the pipeline. This is the responsibility of your Sales Director or MD, as it requires assessing all your salespeople.

- **KPIs**

Each sales person in your team should have a set of relevant KPIs and they should be able to access the information you are using to create or modify them.

KPIs can also be used as a sense check on whether your forecasts are actually realistic and achievable. If your overall business sales targets translate to unrealistic KPIs for individual salespeople, you will need to rethink your targets.

Sales Meetings and Structure

I've always been keener on sport, particularly rugby, than any academic subject. I couldn't wait to leave school and didn't see the point in a lot of what we were being taught. I could read, I could write, I was good at maths and that was enough. When I discovered sales, knew I was good at it and realised that I liked it, I was eager to learn all I could. I started reading and researching the best ways to do things. My old teachers wouldn't have recognised me.

The challenges and the opportunities of selling were what hooked me and I should admit, not having to get up at 4am every day and face whatever the English Channel could throw at me had huge appeal.

I loved every part of sales, particularly the sales meetings when the whole team got together. It was like the meetings our rugby team had. Talking structure, talking plans, talking tactics. As a young and inexperienced sales person I mostly sat and soaked it all up. It felt like the combined wisdom and experience of the senior guys was being poured into me, mixed with practical ways to use it.

GOAL: *To investigate whether you have a regular sales review process.*

DISCOVERY: *What form does your review process take?*

A clear sales process is an essential component of success. Regular sales meetings with a consistent structure to give continuity and focus, is at the heart of the sales management process.

Consider the following:

- Do your managers and their sales teams have regular sales meetings scheduled in their calendars?
- If meetings do happen, how effective are they?
- Are they held regularly or on an ad hoc basis?
- Do they have a clear purpose with an agenda?
- Do attendees understand why they are there and how they contribute to and benefit from them?
- Is there an effective structure to ensure the best use of the time?

You should be very clear about what regular sales meetings can achieve, for your management and the troops on the ground:

- Sales Managers and the Sales Director will be able to identify potential issues early
- Assessment and communication of where the team is in relation to sales targets
- Managers can get a sense of whether they are on track to meet expectations
- Managers can remind the team where the sales function fits into the overall business structure
- Managers can help the team to understand the consequences and impact that unexpected shortfalls or failure to hit targets will have on the rest of the business
- Salespeople have an opportunity to see the bigger picture and their part in it, they can be

motivated by seeing how their activities contribute to the success of the organisation

- Communication of key information to help salespeople improve their performance in relation to products, customers, sales and marketing materials
- Opportunity for feedback from the sales team to management on those issues and any others
- Opportunity for Salespeople to share ideas, knowledge and experiences that can benefit their colleagues
- Opportunity to discuss training and reinforce its importance

ACTIONS:

Managers need to start with the basic principles of effective sales meetings:

Structure - salespeople will know what to expect and it will avoid meetings becoming endless talking-shops

Regularity – reinforces the importance of the meetings, allows attendees to plan their schedules and be prepared with any required documentation

Fact-based - KPIs and metrics are essential for analysis to ensure the meeting is based on facts, rather than conjecture about what is happening in the business

Two-way communication - Managers need to make time to hear what the sales teams think

Follow up - Minutes and action points taken. Actions need to be agreed, with dates and deadlines. Decisions and key points should be documented in the meeting minutes and distributed after the meeting to ensure items are followed up and closed.

The key mechanics of the meetings are:

Structure / Logistics

- Sales meetings must be held regularly to reinforce the fact that they are a part of the fabric of the sales team

- They must be frequent enough to allow issues to be confronted before they become serious

- Held at a time that allows all to attend and give their full attention - Monday morning is better than Friday afternoon

- Attendees should receive an agenda ahead of the meeting to allow them to organise their contribution with no excuse for lack of preparation

- Salespeople should be told in plenty of time what data and analysis they are expected to bring to the meetings

- Meetings should only be cancelled as a last resort - if they are frequently rescheduled for any reason the sales team will not take them seriously and confidence and morale will be eroded

Content

- A review of recent team performance should be a regular item in the meeting and should be placed in the context of the company's overall sales targets

- Appropriate KPIs, reflecting performance of the sales function as a whole, should be used consistently to measure progress towards sales goals

- Sales management should review developments relating to existing products, new products, new features, customers, including feedback from other parts of the business and competitors, new pricing strategies and new competitor products

- Management can introduce new sales and marketing collateral and request feedback on existing materials

- Opportunity for communication upward from the sales team to allow them to express concerns, raise issues and ask questions

- Opportunity for communication in the sales team: sharing customer information, exchange of ideas and tips on product related matters

Performance Management

Consistency is one of the most important words when it comes to sales and sales management, but unfortunately, it's a word that doesn't appear to mean very much to many sales people. As someone who has often fallen into the 'Heroic MD' trap of putting my nose into too many things, I've learned to my cost that the one thing you need to be, is consistent when it comes to managing performance. I like to think I've generally managed to keep most sales people onside with my bouncy 'Tigger' like tendencies, but I know I could have done even better if I'd been more consistent in managing performance, both when things were going well and not so well.

GOAL: *To ensure that you have a transparent, consistent performance management process in place.*

DISCOVERY: *Are the practical components of your performance management system in place and is there provision for training and development where needed?*

Performance management is about making sure that your sales people are doing what they should be doing and doing it well. To meet your expectations, they need to know what is expected of them and the criteria against which they are being measured.

Take an honest look at your performance management process and ask if it meets the basic criteria of being structured, transparent and timely:

Structured: Sales is a process and the performance of a salesperson should be evaluated systematically.

Transparent: Salespeople need to know the exact basis on which they are being assessed to enable them to meet expectations.

Timely: Salespeople should meet one to one with their managers for a review, often enough to ensure that any issues are picked up early, but not so frequently that they have not had time to implement any action points from the previous review.

Reviewing recent activities and results is a large part of the process, but performance management is also about looking forward. A performance review is an opportunity to identify areas where an individual would benefit from personal development. There are three ways to provide that development:

1. **Training:** Related to specific elements of the selling skill set or other focused aspects such as product features and specifications.

2. **Coaching:** An informal, ad hoc approach that can be helpful when a salesperson is having difficulty in a specific area.

3. **Mentoring:** Although sales is a process-driven activity, there is plenty of scope for sales people to customise their approach. The most successful salespeople should be encouraged to share their methods with others, particularly the younger or less experienced members of the team.

These should not just be provided as a quick fix for those falling short of expectations. Performance management should be seen as a positive exercise, even though it is likely to expose performance issues. Your sales people should be open to different or new ideas and be able to accept change. If they are operating in a particular way and need to be coached to perform differently, they must be able to take on the new way of working. An experienced sales person might believe they know all they need to know and will resist change, even if they know they are under threat or underperforming. If a person resists training, coaching and mentoring then their future with your company looks decidedly shaky.

A sales person who is underperforming and continues to approach their prospects in the same way, with the same results, is never going to improve. Your best performers will see a performance review as an opportunity to be recognised for their results and a path to future promotion. If they are not given the opportunity, they will find another employer to fill the gap. The return on investment in performance management and training is high, because it enables the sales team to improve and reach their targets, in addition to increasing your chances of retaining your best employees.

ACTIONS:

Structured process:

Performance review tools, covering all key elements of the sales process, are the basis for the structured assessment approach. A basic performance management template should consist of:

- The salesperson's responsibilities and related goals
- The measures – KPIs - that monitor their performance
- The individual's documented performance for the period under discussion

The review needs hard data: leads generated, meetings arranged and sales achieved. It should also consider the elements that contribute to those numbers including product knowledge and organisational ability. Individual characteristics such as motivation, reliability and ability to cope under pressure, are also significant factors in success. Although an individual's characteristics can be considered as subjective, soft metrics and harder to quantify, they can be measured by attendance at training courses, direct observation by their manager and feedback from customers and peers.

Written documentation is essential to underpin the review. The manager and salesperson should both have the assessment criteria and evidence of performance prior to the review and have it for reference to prevent the discussion drifting into the subjective. After the review, the outcome of the discussion and any action points should be documented and agreed by both parties.

Transparent process:

The single most important aspect of performance management is that the sales person and their manager know and have agreed to the objectives are set for them. Every member of the sales team should know the KPIs against which their performance is to be measured. The

KPIs should be explained when the salesperson first joins the organisation.

Managers must evaluate the results in relation to the KPIs, rewarding success and implementing an action plan with any under-performers to enable them to improve. The purpose of a performance review is to assess achievements versus objectives. Adopting a process like the SMART - Specific, Achievable, Realistic, Timely - approach will help to keep the purpose in focus.

Timely process:

The timing of reviews will vary depending on the nature of your company's products and the associated buying cycle. With a longer buying cycle, less frequent reviews might be appropriate, as it will take longer for the main KPIs to change.

Training:

You should ensure you have a structure in place to deliver the development processes that are essential to boosting the skills of your sales staff. A regular process of instilling knowledge, introducing new techniques and practicing skills is required to keep employees engaged. It will also build and reinforce the skills that will improve their performance and progress their careers.

Coaching:

Salespeople should be following the company's sales process but if they are having difficulties in specific areas, individual coaching should be provided.

Mentoring:

Your less experienced salespeople should be given the opportunity to work alongside your top performing salespeople. Sitting in on client meetings with a top performer in action is a valuable way for them to observe a wealth of skill and experience first hand. It can be a powerful motivator.

Mindset and Skillset

The sales process is an exchange of value. The more value you can build into your offering the quicker your buyer will move to a yes decision. The customer needs to see and believe they are getting more value than they are outlaying for a purchase.

Skillset is very important. You need to learn how to manage and control face-to-face encounters and keep the process within healthy boundaries without losing control of the sales process. These are skills that can be learned and practice is invaluable.

Mindset is equally important. This is your attitude and commitment. The wrong mindset can derail your skillset, but you can improve your attitude with the confidence that practicing your skillset will give you. Skillset and mindset, practice, practice, practice makes perfect.

Dealing with Poor Sales Performance

When your sales staff perform poorly it can affect everything from your bottom line to office morale. It's important to address poor employee performance promptly and develop a strategy for improvement.

Simply telling a sales person to sell more is not sufficient, especially if they don't improve and you decide to terminate their employment. You need to discuss and document their performance issues with them and the steps agreed to help them improve. This provides you with a performance plan that could get your under-performer back on track and will help protect you, if a terminated employee takes legal action against your company.

Collect Proof

Proof of the employee's underperformance: poor sales figures, poor work, poor meeting skills, are needed to support your claim of poor performance and will serve as evidence in the event of a dispute.

Schedule a meeting

Schedule a meeting with the underperforming employee. During the meeting, clarify your expectations, tell them how they are failing to meet those expectations and show them your proof of poor performance.

Let them explain and be consistent with all team members

Allow the employee to explain their poor performance and document it in your notes. If there are significant emotional or personal problems affecting their work, provide information about your company's employee assistance program if you think it's appropriate.

Develop a Plan

Develop a performance improvement plan. The plan should include actionable steps for improvement, a deadline for demonstrated improvement and an outline of the consequences for failing to meet the plan's goals. The plan should be reasonable and aligned to the person's KPIs. Sign the document and ask the sales person to sign it, explaining that by signing, they are agreeing to the contents and the deadline for the expected improvement.

Document the meeting

Write a memo based on your meeting notes highlighting the points of the discussion and the steps the employee has agreed to take to improve. The employee must sign and date it to indicate they have seen and accepted the contents.

Add any relevant notes

Add the notes, performance improvement plan and the performance review memo to the employee's personnel file. Monitor their improvement at regular meetings or take further action as necessary. Discussion with your HR partner can be helpful.

Strategic Planning

'I've worked out that you need to sack 7 of your top 20 customers' was what my new accountant told me after I'd bought my first business. I was a relatively young MD and had just gambled my house to buy a small IT reseller business. He continued: 'Matt, you need a strategic plan to either upsell these clients or get rid of them otherwise you'll be in trouble. They are not in your target market and you're making no margin from them.' He was right and with the threat of losing my house hanging over me, we created a strategic plan. The end result was six clients on far better terms and one lost client - there was a big cheer internally - because the one we lost was very difficult to manage.

GOAL: *Does your company have the information to create a strategic sales plan?*

DISCOVERY: *What are the key elements of strategic sales planning?*

It is the responsibility of the Sales Manager to drive their team to meet their KPIs and hit the numbers. The Sales Manager will typically be responsible for a geographic area or product line and that will be their focus, but sales is no longer just a numbers game with the goal to bang on as many doors and make as many calls as possible. There is now a significant strategic element. Strategic planning is about the bigger picture and is the backdrop for the day-to-day job of selling. The Sales Director, whose role is to look at higher-level issues, is responsible for the strategic sales plan that will set your company up for long-term success.

Strategic planning starts with an evaluation of the key external factors that affect your company. They include:

Size and scope of the market

The Sales Director must have a current picture of the size and scope of the market for your company's products. They need to know how the market is evolving, be aware of the changing needs of your customers and the types of products they want. They must also have a grasp of the overall growth rate of the market to enable them to judge whether your company is gaining or losing market share.

Customers

The Sales Director needs to know how many potential customers there are for your company's products. They must also be able to identify the person with the authority to make purchasing decisions in each of your customers' businesses.

Competitors

It is vital to have a clear understanding of the competitive landscape and the Sales Director must know how many competitors there are and have knowledge of their strengths and weaknesses.

ACTIONS:

Armed with that information, the Sales Director should work with the Sales Managers to construct and direct a team of the right size, with the right skills to sell the right products to take on the competitors.

Translating market intelligence into a sales strategy

An understanding of the size of the market and the number of customers is necessary to evaluate the size of the sales team required to cover the addressable market. Managers will also have to estimate how many prospects each salesperson can realistically handle, but once that is established, the decision can be made to determine how large the sales function needs to be to cover the market.

Evaluating competitors and developing the value proposition

Your business needs to offer products that meet the needs of your customers. A well-informed Sales Director can provide valuable input into the process of providing those products. They will have researched the strengths and weaknesses of competing products and should have produced battlecards analysing the other industry players. They will understand how companies endeavour to stand out within your industry on the basis of quality, price, innovation or service.

The well-informed Sales Director will be able to help develop your company's competitive strategy. They will be able to prioritise and segment customers by: product excellence, operational efficiency, customer service and modify the sales approach accordingly.

Allocating resources

Allocating appropriate resources based on priority and segmentation will help to identify strengths and weaknesses in the sales team. Knowing what is required to sell into the particular segment will highlight skills gaps and shape the strategies to address them through training. Understanding how the market is developing will help to prepare the sales staff to be ahead of the game and not running to catch up.

Reviewing Performance

A top-down strategic view of the market is vital to make meaningful judgements on the performance of your sales team. Without an understanding of the field on which they are playing it will be difficult to assess how well they are doing. Winning new customers in a slow growing, highly competitive market is much more difficult than in a fast expanding, open market. The review will feed in to performance evaluation and remuneration strategy.

Sales and marketing cooperation

A strategic sales strategy based on all these factors should run alongside a complementary marketing strategy. Sales Directors with a truly strategic view will be able to generate ideas about the disruptive marketing approaches that can win market share. They will be able to provide invaluable input to those responsible for generating marketing materials to support the sales function.

Integration with the wider business

There's a naval expression: 'a tight ship (derived from the word taut) is a happy ship'. Roughly translated it means that effectively running an organisation in an orderly and disciplined manner will make it a happy place to be. As it's a naval expression it's implied that everyone will have at least a basic appreciation and respect for what is expected of them and others, and be able to work as a team to get the job done. Unfortunately, sales teams are known for being a touch arrogant and may rudely refer to other areas in a company as 'sales prevention departments'. Of course it's true that if you don't sell anything there won't be any revenue, but a manager or MD who lets their sales team get away with that sort of attitude, and fails to address any potential areas of internal conflict, should plead guilty to 'dereliction of duty'.

GOAL: *To investigate whether your sales force and those who manage it are working effectively with the rest of your organisation.*

DISCOVERY: *Are your salespeople and Sales Director regularly interacting with the other corporate functions and operating as a fully integrated part of your whole business?*

The sales department often seems to be divorced from the rest of a business. If you think this is the case in your business you need to take steps to fix it. Salespeople have the closest and most frequent contact with your customers, with a unique window on what the market thinks of your products and services. It is logical and essential to ensure that this valuable intelligence is shared with the many different departments in your business. Equally, salespeople have a lot to gain from the interaction and cooperation with other business functions.

It is crucial to identify the areas that are the most important for integration and cooperation with sales and discover whether it is happening within your business.

Sales Director:

Leading by example, the Sales Director must forge close cross-functional relationships because strategic planning has to take place in conjunction with other departments to be meaningful. As an example of how important it is, consider:
- If the Sales Director doesn't know about new products they won't be included in the sales forecasts
- To secure the resources they need to meet their targets they will need to work closely with Finance

Sales team and product designers:

Salespeople have to know about the product pipeline to keep customers informed about future offerings. To be completely familiar with the products they are selling, they need to access the best source of information and that is the product designers.

In addition, the product designers should be listening to information from the sales team. Customers and prospects, even those that do not turn into customers, provide honest feedback on the strengths and weaknesses of your company's products. The product developers might believe they have a unique product with specific features designed to appeal to customers, but salespeople can offer market insight into whether competitors are offering superior features or if the value of those features has been over-estimated. The best salesperson in the world depends on the product or service they sell, so it is logical to have their involvement in the design and development.

Sales team and service providers:

The product is only one aspect of the sale; customers are buying a whole package and will judge your business in its totality, including delivery, maintenance/service, help desk, finance and billing. If your customers are not happy with any of the functions, the sales team must offer that feedback to the relevant department.

Sales team and tech experts:

When there is an understanding of how every department contributes to the sale, it allows for other functions to participate. For example, a technical expert could be drafted in to demonstrate the technical aspect of an offering to back up the door-opening salesperson.

Sales and Marketing:

Sales and marketing always need to work closely together. This is particularly true with the growth of content marketing. The sales process has changed to reflect the fact that typically, customers now gather most of the essential information they need before ever speaking to a salesperson. Your customer will have consumed a variety of content marketing materials: case studies, white papers, sales videos, by the time the salesperson joins the process. The salesperson's story must align with the one in your marketing materials.

ACTIONS:

Encouraging interaction, communication and cooperation between sales and other departments is critical.

Depending on the size of your company and the set up of your sales department you may not have a Sales Director. Without a person in that or an equivalent position it will be difficult to encourage the top-level cross-departmental cooperation that will filter down to the level of the salesperson and their peers. If you don't have a Sales Director role, you should consider the disadvantage to your company and the risk involved.

In the absence of a Sales Director, there will be nobody to grasp the size, scope and growth rate of the addressable market and as that information drives decisions on the size and structure of the sales team, there will be nobody to make a credible case to the finance function for the required resources.

At the next level down, cooperation between different organisational functions will happen in both formal and informal contexts.

Formal interactions can take place in training sessions and weekly meetings. One-off training sessions can be arranged for the product team to brief the sales teams on product features and USPs. People from other departments – customer service, marketing - can be invited to speak at weekly sales meetings.

While formal interactions are significant, the whole culture of your organisation should encourage an exchange of information and ideas. Salespeople should want to talk to the marketing team. They should keep themselves up-to-date on marketing output, be familiar with the latest white papers and case studies. They should visit the company website regularly to view the content that their prospective customers will already have seen. They should want to make friends in the tech team so that they can call on an expert for back up in a customer pitch.

Forcing salespeople to engage in these informal interactions is difficult. Instilling those values in your business starts with hiring the right people and explaining what is expected of them when they join. A good attitude that creates a positive culture is reinforced by your remuneration policy and by rewarding people for exhibiting the right behaviour.

The sales teams need to work to gain respect from the other corporate functions by demonstrating their professionalism, consistently following a sales methodology and working in a defined structure. They need to lay to rest the view of the maverick sales person flying by the seat of their pants in an undisciplined way. If the sales team can do that, others in your organisation will have a much clearer idea of how they can contribute to the sales effort and will want to be involved.

Conclusion

When I decided to write this book I didn't really know how long it would be. I knew I had a lot of information that I wanted to share, but until I set out my structure and started to fill in the sections I had no idea what it would look like. As I went along, more ideas, more experience and more knowledge appeared, begging to be included. I couldn't and didn't put everything in. I've tried to keep it to the logical sequences and important things to help you get your business where you want it to be.

Writing and publishing this book is the best way for me to collaborate with the most people I can. I've been the beneficiary of so many great thinkers and sales people willing to share what they know with me, that I wanted to share it with you. When I hear the story of someone's road to success, it inspires me and motivates me to do better.

After more than 25 years in the sales business and owning my own companies, I know only too well that most businesses will hit a wall at some point, where their future potential exceeds their current abilities.

The reasons for this are as varied, as there are fish in the sea, but if you have the appetite for giving your business a thorough service, you'll find out what's not working and with a little adjustment where it needs it you'll be able to get back to where you want to be. Sales really isn't rocket science, but I would argue that there is a science to sales. It most definitely isn't magic, although it can seem like magic if you don't know why something works. I can't stress enough the importance of consistency and process.

If you know what you do, know how you do it and know who does it, then document it, teach it to all your team and you will be able to repeat, repeat, repeat your way to the bank.

My company, Sales Plus Profit, was set up to fix sales and profit challenges wherever they raise their ugly heads. We have a great track record and it's the most satisfying work, but I've also become increasingly aware that a lot of companies are downsizing and reigning in their spending. Unfortunately this often means that it's heads down and work as you always have in the hope that things will change. They won't. If there's something fundamentally adrift in your vision, people, process or management you will do the same things and get the same results. At times like this, it's vital to take stock and really look at what's going on in your business. Don't be afraid of the assessment and what you find out. This is the key to your future success.

Everything in my methodology shows you what to look for, where to look for it and how to fix it. I've never liked the feeling that money, or lack of it, could prevent progress and I've attempted to address that by putting what I know in this easy to read book.

As I mentioned earlier, there are a million different things that could create a challenge for your business and probably a million different ways you could handle it. I believe consistency is the key to managing the unexpected, because with consistent process and focus, the unexpected doesn't exist. There should not be anything in your competitive marketplace that you don't know about and you should already be armed with a strategy, ready to action, if and when you need it.

I hope you get a lot out of the material here. I fully believe in it and practice this stuff every day in my own business. I still get an incredible buzz out of working with all sorts of businesses, with all sorts of challenges. Some are struggling, some want to increase their efficiency, some just want to simplify what they do. It's a privilege to be on the journey with them to achieve whatever it is they're aiming for. There's not much better feeling than helping to make things better for everyone involved.

At the beginning I asked the question: 'Who is this book for?'

The simple answer: It's for anyone in business.

Including:

- The CEO who wants to stimulate growth

- The MD who wants to recalibrate areas in their business

- The Business Leader who wants to have a high performing sustainable sales team

- The Sales Leader who wants to increase the efficiency of their team

- The Sales Executive who wants to fine tune their personal performance and build their knowledge for future promotion

- The Sales recruit in their first job, still green around the gills, eager to learn how to make a difference

- The Investor who wants to know why their investment is not quite what they hoped and what they can do to change that

Or perhaps it's for you, if you're happy with your business performance, but know that you don't have the consistency to sustain your results long term. Challenging complacency is healthy and a good way to ensure your business stays on top form.

My business is your business and if you've read this and have questions you'd like me to answer or you just want to tell me how you're getting on, I'm always happy to have a chat. You can contact me via my website, LinkedIn or on the Sales Plus Profit website.

www.mattgarman.com

www.salesplusprofit.com

https://www.linkedin.com/in/matt-garman-2807794/

Lightning Source UK Ltd.
Milton Keynes UK
UKHW02f2319280218
318657UK00009B/427/P